COSMETICS, FASHIONS, AND
THE EXPLOITATION OF WOMEN

COSMETICS
FASHIONS
AND THE
EXPLOITATION
OF WOMEN

JOSEPH HANSEN
EVELYN REED
MARY-ALICE WATERS

PATHFINDER

New York   London   Montreal   Sydney

ISBN 978-0-87348-659-0
Library of Congress Catalog Card Number 85-63365
Manufactured in the United States of America

First edition, 1986
Fourteenth printing, 2011

Cover artwork: Nancy Spero, *Athena of Aegina*, 1991 (detail) of 20″ x 110″
handpainting and collage on paper. Photograph courtesy of the artist and
the Josh Baier Gallery, New York City. Nancy Spero lives and works in
New York City. Her exhibitions and installations have appeared in galleries
in New York, Tokyo, Frankfurt, Derry, and many other cities around the
world.
Cover design: Toni Gorton
The passages from Russell Lynes, *The Tastemakers*, are © 1954 and
reprinted by permission of the author.

Pathfinder

www.pathfinderpress.com
E-mail: pathfinder@pathfinderpress.com

Contents

About the authors

Joseph Hansen (1910–1979) was a longtime revolutionary journalist and leader of the Socialist Workers Party in the United States. He joined the socialist movement in 1934. During the 1950s Hansen was editor of the *Militant* newsweekly and of the *International Socialist Review*.

Hansen visited Cuba in 1960 and helped launch the Fair Play for Cuba Committee upon his return. His writings on the evolution of the Cuban revolution are collected in *Dynamics of the Cuban Revolution*, published by Pathfinder.

Evelyn Reed (1905–1979) joined the socialist movement in 1940 and was a leader of the Socialist Workers Party for many years. Her pioneering work, *Woman's Evolution*, published by Pathfinder, has been translated into five languages. She is also author of *Problems of Women's Liberation* and *Sexism and Science*.

A participant in the women's liberation struggles of the 1960s and 1970s, Reed was a founding member of the Women's National Abortion Action Coalition and the National Organization for Women.

Mary-Alice Waters is a leader of the U.S. Socialist Workers Party. Influenced by the unfolding revolution in Cuba and the mass battle against Jim Crow in the United States, she joined the communist movement in 1962.

Formerly an editor of the *Militant,* she is currently editor of *New International,* a magazine of Marxist politics and theory.

Waters is author of *Women's Liberation and the Socialist Revolution* and *Che Guevara and the Fight for Socialism Today,* and editor of *How Far We Slaves Have Come!* by Nelson Mandela and Fidel Castro, *Rosa Luxemburg Speaks, Communist Continuity and the Fight for Women's Liberation,* and other works.

The capitalist ideological offensive against women today

by Mary-Alice Waters

In 1954 a sharp debate broke out in the pages of the *Militant*, the weekly newspaper that reflects the views of the Socialist Workers Party in the United States. The controversy, surprisingly enough, was over the relation of the marketing of cosmetics and fashions to the oppression of women. *Militant* editor Joseph Hansen, using the pen name Jack Bustelo, wrote an item headlined "Sagging Cosmetic Lines Try a Face Lift." This book opens with Bustelo's article. It is a lively, short exposé of the ways in which the owners of the big cosmetics companies try to manipulate women's insecurities and fears to sell commodities and rake in massive profits.

The article prompted a rapid letter of protest to the editor, charging that Bustelo was ridiculing women. The reader said Bustelo was challenging the right of working-class women to strive for "some loveliness and beauty in their lives." Bustelo's response in the *Militant* letters column evoked a further round of protests.

It soon became clear that the substantive political questions emerging from this at-first seemingly minor controversy merited a more extensive discussion than could be aired in the pages of the *Militant*. Since many of the contributors to the letters column were also members of the Socialist Workers Party, the SWP's Political Committee decided to open an organized debate in the party's internal *Discussion Bulletin*.

This book, *Cosmetics, Fashions, and the Exploitation of Women*, is drawn from the record of this debate, which came to be known in the history of the Socialist Workers Party as the "Bustelo controversy."

While the expanding production and marketing of cosmetics hardly seems to be a topic of great importance, this discussion was neither frivolous, nor an academic sociological dispute. It was one expression of the struggle to maintain a proletarian party and Marxist program throughout the cold war and anticommunist witch-hunt of the early 1950s.

Three decades later, many women will recognize that most of the questions discussed here—and the social pressures they reflect—are still with us. Radical-minded working people, male and female, will find the material collected in this book of particular interest; it will aid them in understanding the political situation in the United States in the 1980s, which is marked by a reactionary and brutal economic, social, political, and ideological offensive by the employers and their government. The letters and articles that make up this collection provide an instructive example of how the class values and norms of the wealthy are foisted on working people and find expression even within the most conscious layers of the working-class movement, especially during periods of political reaction and retreat.

The record of this discussion is also an education in leadership methods in the workers' movement. It shows how the SWP leadership, in an objective and pedagogical way, sought to clarify the underlying issues, thus helping party members and supporters to be more conscious of and arm themselves against the prevailing pressures.

Post–World War II reaction

At the end of World War II, the U.S. rulers came out on top of the imperialist heap, with their main capitalist rivals devastated. The postwar workers' upsurge in Western Europe was crushed. The 1945–46 strike wave in the United States ended in a stalemate. These factors established the preconditions for a quarter century of capitalist economic expansion during which broad layers of U.S. working people were able to wrest significant concessions from the bosses.

At the same time, however, the world system of imperialist domination had been weakened. While the imperial masters were fighting each other, the masses of colonial slaves rebelled. Revolutionary struggles for independence exploded throughout Asia and Africa. Despite enormous losses and devastation, the Soviet Union emerged victorious over German imperialism. The workers and peasants of Eastern Europe and China put an end to landlord-capitalist rule in vast new areas of the globe.

The response of the imperialist powers to these mortal blows was to launch and then expand the cold war against the Soviet Union and its new allies. The imperialists attempted to militarily crush the national liberation forces in Korea and Vietnam. Some individuals at top levels of the U.S. government gave serious consideration to using nuclear weapons against the people of those two countries and thus to repeating the horrors inflicted on the civilian populations of Hiroshima and Nagasaki a few years earlier.

In the United States, the domestic side of the cold war was an anticommunist witch-hunt. It was aimed at destroying the unity and combativity of the industrial unions born in the great labor upsurge of the 1930s. It sought to turn back the postwar surge in the fight for Black civil rights. It was intended to sow fear, division, and demoralization among all those fighting for social progress. Through the witch-hunt, the employers sought to assure the conditions of labor "peace" and political passivity necessary for an extended period of intensified exploitation of working people and accelerated capitalist accumulation.

The witch-hunt was at its peak as the 1950s began to unfold. The depoliticization of working-class fighters in the unions deepened. There was less and less motion in the labor movement around social questions and no extensive political life independent of the employers' parties. As a result of these conditions, the membership of the Socialist Workers Party—as well as that of the Communist Party and other organizations on the left—declined sharply and rapidly. Socialists became more and more isolated politically. The SWP was forced into a largely semisectarian existence; its activity could no longer be based on an organized political life as part of a working-class vanguard within the industrial unions.

That was the political context in which the debate over cosmetics, fashions, and the exploitation of women broke out in the SWP. It registered the impact of the U.S. rulers' political offensive to divide workers and weaken their class consciousness.

During World War II women had been incorporated into the labor force in larger numbers than ever before. Even more importantly, they were hired to perform many jobs from which women had previously been excluded. This broadened the social and political horizons of tens of millions of women who had formerly been trapped in the stultifying confines of the home or employed only in jobs traditionally hiring female labor. This also brought irreversible changes in the way that both women and men thought about women's place in society. When the war was over, there were millions of women and men who wanted to maintain these newly conquered social and economic relations.

For the employing class, however, increasing economic independence and social equality for women is incompatible with intensified superexploitation of female labor power. Hence, the deliberate promotion during postwar years of the "feminine mystique," as it later came to be known. This extensive political and ideological campaign was aimed at rolling back the changes in attitudes about women's proper role. It was promoted in order to reinforce the idea that women—whether or not they are part of the labor force—should first and foremost be wives, mothers, and housekeepers. Thus women should accept employment at lower wages and under worse conditions. Women should spend less time on union activity or political concerns and should take less interest in them.

Women were not the only target of the rulers' ideological campaign. This reactionary assault, waged through the mass media, schools, and churches, was directed toward reversing the attitudes of both sexes concerning women's social role. But its impact on women was different. To a large extent women, like other oppressed layers of capitalist society, internalize the pressures on them. They place limitations on themselves, often unconsciously. They accept the socially prescribed roles, and, in fact, often promote the conditions that perpetuate their own oppression.

Through the "cosmetics" debate that took place among members of the Socialist Workers Party, we get a glimpse of the diverse, if not so subtle, ways in which the postwar period of reaction affected even women and men who were socialists and conscious champions of women's liberation. We see how the pressures affected the way people thought about themselves.

Changes in women's social conditions since 1950

Since the early 1950s, of course, there have been extensive changes in the economic and social conditions facing women in the United States. The domestic and international political situation has been vastly altered, as well.

Most importantly, the accelerated expansion of capitalism in the postwar years brought with it an even greater incorporation of women into the labor market than during World War II. In 1950, 33.9 percent of women sixteen years of age and over were in the labor force. By 1960 that figure had risen to 37.7 percent. In 1970 it was 43.3 percent. And by 1983, more than half of all working-age women—52.9 percent—were in the labor force. During that thirty-three-year period, the percentage increase of women who were in the labor market was slightly more than the percentage increase during the seventy years between 1890 and 1960!

Women today account for 43 percent of the labor force, as compared with 29 percent in 1950. This marks a qualitative advance in the economic independence of women and consequently a change in their social status.

It is also important, however, to take a look at the changes in *where* women are employed. Two of the most carefully promoted myths are the notions that working women have generally "escaped" from industrial jobs, and that this represents a rising economic and social status for women. The reality is far more complex. The most important advances for women—although directly involving only a small percentage of women—have been precisely those that have integrated them more deeply into the most strongly organized, predominantly male, sectors of the industrial working class.

The expansion of the labor market in general since 1950 has been marked by an increase in clerical, commercial, and other nonindustrial jobs relative to those in industrial production. Since the influx of women into the labor market has been much more rapid than that of men, the percentage of employed women working industrial jobs has declined.

Over this same thirty-five-year period, however, there has also been a much greater incorporation of women into industrial production. *In fact, the percentage of industrial workers who are women has significantly risen since World War II.* Moreover, since the early 1970s women have fought their way into many types of jobs from which they had previously been excluded. The categories used by government statistical bureaus make it difficult to obtain fully reliable figures, but the trend is nonetheless clear.

For example, while the total number of men categorized as "blue-collar workers" increased by 29 percent between 1950 and 1981, the number of women in such jobs went up by some 61.5 percent; this increased the percentage of workers who are women in such job categories from 15.4 percent to 18.6 percent over that thirty-one-year period.

The increase is even more noticeable in the subcategories of "operatives" (assemblers, punch- and stamping-press operators, welders, sewing-machine operators, truck drivers, fork-lift operators, etc.) and "craft" workers (carpenters, electricians, sheet-metal workers, tool-and-die makers, mechanics, etc.).

In craft positions, the gains for women are especially striking, since they had been largely frozen out of these jobs until recently. The number of men holding such jobs went up by 58.5 percent between 1950 and 1981; the number of women leaped by 327 percent. The percentage of women in the crafts is still small, but it has grown from 2.5 percent in 1950 to 6.3 percent in 1981.

Among operatives, the number of men went up by 8 percent between 1950 and 1981, while the number of women grew by 35 percent; this increased the proportion of women in such production jobs from 27.4 percent to 32.3 percent.

The number of women mine workers grew from 0.7 percent of miners in 1972 to 2.2 percent in 1981. Among underground miners, the percentage of women hired went from almost zero in 1973–74 to between 8 and 10 percent in the first five years of the 1980s.[1]

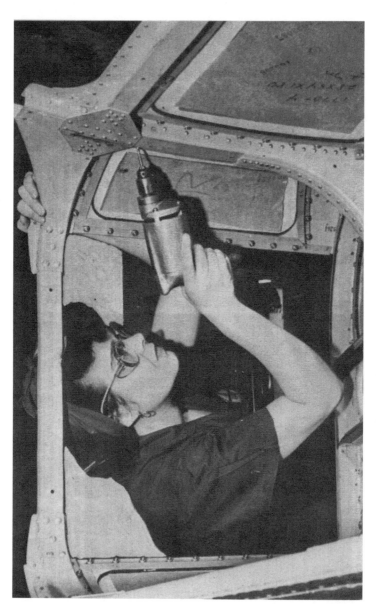

Woman working on aircraft during World War II.

Women in the industrial unions

If we look at the position of women as part of the organized labor movement, a similarly complex picture emerges.

The level of unionization of women workers has declined over the past several decades as part of the overall sharp decline in union membership. This fact tells only part of the story, however.

The gains for women in industrial production jobs previously off-limits to them—whether in mining, steel, auto, or whatever—have usually meant integration into the industrial unions in a qualitatively new way. Probably the best example is the employment of women in coal mining and the growing role of women in the United Mine Workers union. Women have been fighting their way into jobs such as coal mining. This is precisely because unions such as the UMWA have won contracts that guarantee higher average wages and better benefits than women can find in traditional "female" occupations. Moreover, women are guaranteed wages and conditions equal to male co-workers in the same job categories. Women who have busted into these industries are often among the most conscious unionists. Many have learned through their own experiences why class solidarity and organization are so indispensable. They know that without union protection they would not stand a chance against the bosses' attempts to divide the work force and turn other workers against them.

Women in the industrial unions, of course, still have to fight discrimination, prejudice, sexual harassment on the job, and "reclassification" schemes to downgrade their wages and conditions and those of other, more recently hired workers. Women often have to help their union brothers learn that sex discrimination weakens the entire labor movement.

But it is precisely by fighting their way into such jobs that women can have an impact on the social conditions that keep the value of their labor power substantially lower than that of men. It is in such industrial union jobs that women are in the best position to develop mutual respect and confidence with male co-workers, gain self-confidence and class consciousness, and affect the attitudes of both men and women about women's role in society.

A woman who works on an assembly line has a different relationship to the men around her than a woman who works as a secretary. And both are in a qualitatively different economic and social situation vis-à-vis men than a woman who remains outside the labor market altogether.

Thus, the changes in the employment statistics for women over the last thirty-five years, and the changes in where women work, codify *social* advances affecting tens of millions of women and men.

Other changes important to women's social position also occurred during the postwar period. For the first time ever, advances in medical science gave women access to birth control methods that were relatively safe and certain, and that were under their own control.

Educational levels rose in general, and women won broader access to job training programs and higher education.

Increasing labor productivity and capitalism's competitive expansion into new sectors of commodity production and distribution created a mass market in the imperialist countries for household appliances and prepared foods. While women have hardly escaped from their domestic slavery, their work load has been eased. A wide range of such commodities have now become incorporated into the historically determined—and changing—value of labor power, to that extent raising the living standards of workers and their families.

An insoluble contradiction

Since the beginning of the industrial revolution in the eighteenth century, capitalist expansion and the lash of competition have dictated the incorporation of larger and larger numbers of women into the labor force. This is so because capital always seeks to incorporate into the work force large numbers of workers in oppressed social categories (in this case women), the value of whose labor power under capitalism is less than that of others. This is a key way in which the employers drive down the overall average value of labor power by heightening competition among workers for jobs.

The development of capitalism, however, creates real—and ultimately insoluble—contradictions for the exploiting class. The capitalists' increasing purchase of women's capacities as wage laborers inevitably brings in its wake greater economic independence for women. It contributes to further disintegration of the family, and expands the need for the household appliances and prepared foods noted above. These factors, in turn, tend to raise the value of women's labor power, to raise the wages they can command in the labor market on average, other things being equal.[2]

Through their experiences in the work force and the unions, women in growing numbers also begin to think in broader social terms and to act as political beings. They become increasingly class conscious. They play an expanding role in struggles by the labor movement that can wrest higher wages from the employers and social programs from the capitalist government, thus pushing up the value of labor power for the entire working class.

These were the kinds of economic and social developments that took place in the decades of the post–World War II capitalist expansion, weakening the foundations on which the entire edifice of women's oppression is built. As these objective preconditions combined with the political changes of the 1950s and 1960s—above all, the civil rights and anti-Vietnam War movements—the "second wave" of feminism exploded onto the scene. As a result of the women's liberation struggles since the end of the 1960s, further broad advances have taken place in women's attitudes toward themselves and their place in society, as well as in the views of men on these matters.

Rulers' reaction against gains by women

The period of accelerated post–World War II capitalist expansion came to an end in the mid-1970s. As this took place, the shifts in the economic and social conditions of women, and the changing attitudes and expectations accompanying them, increasingly clashed with the economic interests— that is, the profits—of the U.S. ruling class. This conflict lies beneath the political and ideological campaign directed against women's rights that we are now living through, just as a similar conflict led to the reactionary promotion of the "feminine mystique" in the late 1940s and 1950s.

Today the employers are once again making a concerted political effort to roll back, or at least slow down, some of the changes in consciousness about women's place in society. They are taking aim at concrete gains won through hard struggle in the 1960s and 1970s, such as abortion rights and affirmative action programs.

The goal of the bosses and their government is not to drive women out of the labor force, but to undermine their class consciousness and political self-confidence. The goal is to make women more willing to acquiesce in attacks on wages, working conditions, social services, affirmative action programs, and equality on the job. In this way, the employers are attempting to hold back the increase in the value of women's labor power (and thereby that of the class as a whole), and to enforce greater discipline and "productivity" by imposing speedup and more dangerous working conditions.

These attacks on women's rights are part of a broader offensive that the U.S. capitalist class has been waging for more than a decade. The target is all working people, and all those whose race, sex, language, or national origin is used by the ruling class to single them out for superexploitation and special oppression. The employers are determined to fundamentally shift the relationship of forces between capital and labor that was established following the post-World War II strike wave.

This intensifying capitalist offensive began with the 1974–75 world recession and picked up steam with the 1980–82 recession. It is directed against the wages, job conditions, democratic rights, and organizations of the working class. It is aimed at heading off progress toward political independence by the working class—toward any notion that labor should develop and fight for its own positions on social and political questions, independent of and opposed to those of the bosses and bosses' parties.

This offensive has been registered in a rightward shift of the entire bipartisan structure of capitalist politics in the United States. It has been accompanied by a sustained ideological offensive aimed at dividing the working class more deeply between employed and unemployed, and along the lines of race, sex, age, "skill levels," language, and national origin. A special goal has been to reverse gains won by Blacks and women, who over the previous period fought their way through some of the barriers that keep them confined to second-class status in capitalist society in general, and within the labor force in particular.

Parallel to this domestic offensive has been an escalation of U.S. aggression abroad, especially in Central America and the Caribbean. As part of the preparations for war, there has been an enormous increase in U.S. military spending. We have seen a constant barrage of anticommunist propaganda, directed above all against Nicaragua, Cuba, and the Salvadoran freedom fighters, but also against Angola, Vietnam, the South African and Palestinian peoples. This has been accompanied by a domestic spy hunt and antiunion "industrial security" campaign. Through the concerted political drive on all these fronts, Wall Street and Washington are trying to bludgeon and con the U.S. working class into believing that *their* foreign policy is in *our* interests.

One result of this sustained economic and political offensive, with all its reactionary ideological offshoots, has been a deepening class polarization in the United States. Not everyone is suffering from the policies that the employers are putting into effect. To the contrary, tens of millions of individuals in middle-class and professional layers are *benefiting* from these policies. Some layers of the working class have also improved their situation—even if the insecurities and pressures that are common to their class also bear down on them. To varying degrees, all these social layers are being pulled to the right politically.

On the other hand, the big majority of workers and working farmers are taking stiffer and stiffer blows. The bosses' offensive has run into resistance, however. There has been opposition to two-tier wage scales, bank foreclosures on struggling farmers, and U.S. military intervention in Central America. Working people have mobilized in defense of Black rights. Struggles have been fought around women's rights, and immigrants' rights.

All of these are labor issues—issues on which the labor movement must have its own policies and defend its own class interests and those of its allies. All are questions on which there is reflection, concern, and a growing willingness to take action on the part of workers. Broad and growing sectors of working people—on the farms and in the factories—are becoming aware that there are interconnections among these many battlefronts.

So far, defeats and setbacks for working people continue to outnumber victories, and the bosses and their politicians retain the initiative. But that has not put a stop to resistance. To the contrary, the willingness and desire of working people to fight back continues to assert itself.

The class polarization and the experiences that are generating it give an impulse to the politicization and radicalization of the most combative workers. But these same developments also embolden rightist proponents of national-chauvinist, racist, anti-Semitic, antiwoman, and antiunion prejudices, as well as other reactionary ideas.

This is the political context in which we need to place the current attacks on women's rights by the employers and their government.

Bosses reinforce antiwoman prejudices

When the bosses go on a stepped-up offensive to shift the relationship of forces in their favor, they play every card in the deck—war and the threat of military aggression abroad; more naked use of the cops and courts at home (whether against Blacks, immigrant workers, farmers, or strikers); massive cuts in social services; tax hikes; union busting and concession contracts. At the same time, they wage a political campaign to justify their course as being in the interests of "all of us." They talk about "equality of sacrifice," the "national interest," "labor-management cooperation," and "common cultural values."

Within this framework, the rulers single out special targets as part of their broad frontal assault. One of these is always the progressive changes taking place in women's social status. The employers are aiming at the advances of working-class women especially, but the barrage is necessarily directed against all women. The second sex must be taught to know its place.

The attack on women's rights is fundamental to the success of the capitalist offensive. Discrimination against women is one of the most important ways in which the rulers work to deepen divisions within the working class. Its acceptance helps the bosses keep the labor movement shackled to a narrow trade union perspective, instead of thinking in broader social terms and acting politically to advance the interests of the oppressed and exploited. The perpetuation of women's subordinate status is one more obstacle along the road to independent working-class political action.

The employers aim to undermine working-class women's consciousness of themselves *as workers, as part of the working class,* and instead to heighten their consciousness of themselves as women—not in the feminist sense, but in all the retrograde ways that are drummed into women from childhood. The employing class seeks to reinforce the prejudices about women's proper place and domestic role. It seeks to convince women that they *want* to be dependent on a man, with the second-class status that entails.

Such prejudices, and the ways women internalize them, go back millennia. But the rise and development of capitalism progressively undermines them, as it forces women out of the home and off the farm and pushes them as individuals into the labor market—with all the brutality inherent in the capitalist mode of production.

The capitalists' offensive against women's rights is not aimed at driving women out of the work force. That is historically precluded. The percentage of wage and salaried workers who are female has been rising, from one plateau to another, ever since the beginning of the industrial revolution. Instead, the aim is to make women more vulnerable to increased exploitation. The goal is not to push women *out* of the labor market but to push them *down*—to jobs with fewer paid holidays, more piece work, less safety, shorter lunch breaks, less union protection, and lower wages.

Women have always made up an important component of the pool of unemployed workers that Marx called the industrial reserve army of labor. This reserve army never disappears under capitalism, even in the best of times. But in a period of capitalist stagnation such as we have lived through over the last decade, the owners of capital need to

Women in a variety of "nontraditional" jobs.

expand this army of the unemployed in order to intensify competition among workers and thus drive down wages. Hundreds of thousands of women workers were forced into its ranks during the 1980–82 recession, eroding some of the employment gains they had previously won.

The bosses' ideological campaign seeks to reinforce the idea among both sexes that women are "natural" recruits to this reserve army. They are "normally" only marginal workers, temporary workers, part-time workers, home workers. Women are only a "second" wage earner in the family. In periods of rising joblessness, there are always assertions by ruling-class "opinion molders" that unemployment statistics are artificially high, since women should not really be counted as unemployed in the same way as men, who are considered the main breadwinners. This propaganda is aimed at convincing women to accept, with less resistance and resentment, temporary unemployment, or new jobs at lower wages. All this is true despite the increase in female heads of household, a trend that will continue as the evolution of capitalism continues to disintegrate the family.

The capitalists want women to blame themselves, not the social relations of production, for the economic and social problems they confront every day. The goal is to make women feel guilty that their children are being permanently damaged by "abandonment" in child-care facilities (if they exist), or are being turned into lonely latch-key delinquents. Rather than demanding—as a *right*—both child-care facilities and equal access to high-paying jobs previously barred to them, women are pushed toward being grateful for any job, at any wage.

Part of the rulers' strategy is also to deepen race divisions. They seek to break down solidarity and intensify competition between women workers who are fighting their way into nontraditional jobs and Black workers, who constitute a large proportion of the politically more conscious, vanguard layers of the working class. Since women are getting jobs that men "ought" to have, they are alleged to be responsible for the high rate of unemployment of Black males. The employers also attempt to pit white women and Black women against each other along similar lines.

Even the notion that backward, prejudiced men are the source of women's problems is accorded a favored niche in the employers' propaganda arsenal as an alternative to the truth that the capitalist system is responsible for perpetuating the oppression of women.

Because the advances in women's status in the 1960s and 1970s were so broad, and the changes in consciousness so sweeping, the counteroffensive against women's rights in the last few years has been all the more concerted. It has taken numerous forms:

• The defeat of the Equal Rights Amendment.

• The onslaught against abortion rights—from the withholding of government funds; to the bombing of clinics; to the propaganda, day in and day out, that abortion is murder, murder, murder. State, local, and federal legislation and court rulings have placed more and more restrictions on abortion rights, and government officials are seeking to make even deeper inroads.

• The concerted drive to roll back affirmative action gains, to foster the "white-male" backlash against Blacks and women.

• Glorification of the family, built around the theme of a woman's special fulfillment of herself as a mother. Supermom is in. She often works a full-time job. That is accepted. But it's only when she comes home, we are told, that her real responsibilities, and her true possibilities for fulfillment, begin. Supermom makes sure her kids—and husband—don't suffer too much for her selfish absorption in her own life. And, deep down, she has a lot of doubts about whether she's doing the right thing. Isn't this "new woman" wonderful?

How many guilt-tripping articles with that reactionary message have been published in the last few years?

Decline of the women's movement

The counteroffensive to roll back the gains women have made has been registered in a decline of the women's movement. Since 1977 the National Organization for Women (NOW) has been turned more and more into an electoralist appendage of the capitalist two-party system. The thousands of small circles of feminist activists that sprang up in the early 1970s have disappeared. The few groups that have survived concentrate largely on specific interests such as women's health clinics or art. Others have been drawn into reactionary campaigns demanding more cops as an answer to the continuing reality of rape, or calling for censorship laws as the way to deal with pornography.

The last time a sizable women's rights action occurred in the United States was 1978. That was the 100,000-strong July 9, 1978, march on Washington called by NOW to demand an extension of the deadline for ERA ratification. There has been no women's liberation action of similar size or impact since then. This is true despite the potential that existed for ongoing mass mobilizations around the ERA and the growing desire of women to act in defense of abortion rights.

That situation will not continue indefinitely. There is growing pressure for a change. There are already indications of a pickup in organized protests responding to the escalating attacks on women's right to abortion.

But the fact remains that there has been no mass, fighting women's movement in the streets or anywhere else for some years. The kind of mass-action movement from which women gain self-confidence as they fight to change things that vitally affect their lives; the kind of action movement through which women learn how to mobilize millions to fight for their rights—that kind of movement does not exist today. The women's liberation forces are on the defensive, not the offensive.

This situation is not unique to the United States. It is a phenomenon that, to varying degrees, marks virtually all capitalist countries where the women's liberation movement had a significant impact in the 1970s. The reasons for this decline are fundamentally the same everywhere. It is one of the fruits of the incapacity of the labor officialdom to mount an effective fight back against the capitalist austerity drive that began with the 1974–75 worldwide recession. Prospects for advancing the fight for women's liberation are not independent of the historic course of the working-class movement, even if women's rights battles can and do surge ahead on occasion—as they did in the early 1970s—and help show the way forward.

All the conservatizing pressures described above have been mounting for nearly a decade now. And they have borne down with a special weight on women. This is not an argument for pessimism about the future; to the contrary, there are some small signs of new struggles on the horizon. It is merely a statement of fact about the past ten years. Moreover, it explains a number of significant and well-documented phenomena that mirror the enforced social and political retreat of women: the sharp increase in childbearing among women in their thirties; the rise in teenage pregnancy rates; the flight by many liberals, including prominent feminists, from an active and outspoken defense of affirmative action quotas for women and Blacks.

Women in industry

Women who are full-time industrial workers and part of the organized labor movement are in the best position to resist the conservatizing pressures that all women are subjected to by the economic, political, and ideological offensive of the ruling class. The reason is simple. The fundamental line of division, of deepening cleavage, is *a class polarization*. Not all women—and not all women who work—are hit by the offensive with equal force and in the same ways. Not only the economic squeeze, but also the necessity to fight back weigh more heavily on working-class women. The reactionary ideological and political offensive of the employers has less fertile ground in which to take root in the working class in general than among middle-class layers.

Women who are industrial workers and union members have a degree of self-confidence that comes from knowing that they can sell their labor power and survive. They are not so economically dependent on a man, and this gives them a greater element of independence in making important decisions that affect their lives. Moreover, they have acquired at least the beginning of working-class consciousness through understanding that they have a better chance at improving wages and working conditions by joining together with fellow workers to defend themselves against the employer. Moreover, despite the bosses' attempts to foster animosities toward them by male workers, women in industry frequently work alongside men in job situations where each depends on the other and relations of mutual respect and confidence can develop.

While women who are industrial workers are less susceptible to right-wing demagogy and reactionary "solutions" to their problems, however, they are nonetheless not immune. They are constantly fighting the bosses' attempts to convince them and their male co-workers that they are not really workers; that being part of the labor force is only a passing moment in women's lives; that the really important thing for them is that they will leave the labor force to raise a family; or that, having already left the labor market to raise a family, they are now past their prime, and should be glad to find a boss "willing" to employ them.

This kind of reactionary propaganda—in a period of working-class political retreat—affects even the most politically conscious women and men. That is why it is helpful to look back at the 1950s and learn from history. It is useful to see how the reactionary offensive against women's rights in that period found an echo inside the Socialist Workers Party. It helps in understanding some of the pressures today, and arms us to deal with them more consciously.

The 'Bustelo controversy'

At the end of 1953 the Socialist Workers Party—under the pressure of the cold war witch-hunt conditions—suffered one of the deepest splits in its history. The split cut through the basic cadre of the party, taking 25 percent of the National Committee and some 20 percent of the membership.

The "Bustelo controversy" erupted in the SWP a few months later. In the *Militant* article referred to at the beginning of this introduction, Bustelo noted that a recession was cutting into the cosmetics industry's profits, since women who were unemployed were buying fewer of its products. The merchants of "beauty," he explained, had announced their plans to revive profits through a calculated campaign to con and terrify women into buying more cosmetics.

Bustelo wrote: "The Toilet Goods Association reports that after thirteen years of steady gains, cosmetics manufacturers' sales suddenly plunged in the first quarter of 1954—right when unemployment took a steep jump." In response, he explained, the big cosmetics dealers were projecting "Operation Big Push." "'Toni, for example, has announced its third new cosmetic in three months, a face cream that no words can describe except Deep Magic.'"

Bustelo went on to explain how the owners of these capitalist enterprises exploit women's insecurities to try to make them buy cosmetics.

The letters of outrage and indignation began to arrive on the *Militant* editor's desk. "Beauty is predominantly monopolized by the wealthy," one reader said. "The wealthy are beautiful because the workers are wretched." Working-class women strive for beauty, this reader argued, and this "has a progressive aspect" because "it is part of the rebellion of women against a position which denies to them part of their rights as human beings."

Bustelo replied with a short, to-the-point letter on beauty, class society, and historical materialism. "I do not believe," he wrote, "that 'beauty is predominantly monopolized by the wealthy,' and that the 'wealthy are beautiful because the workers are wretched.'

"It appears to me that you might just as well say that 'morality is predominantly monopolized by the wealthy,' and that the 'wealthy are moral because the workers are immoral.'" The standards of beauty, Bustelo pointed out, like the standards of morality, are determined in the final analysis by the ruling class. And, he added, "I think most of the customs and norms of capitalist society are ridiculous and even vicious, including the customs and norms of wealthy bourgeois women."

Bustelo's reply provoked further outraged responses, which are reprinted in this collection. Several readers argued that the use of cosmetics was a basic economic necessity for a working woman to get a job and keep a man. Thus, the SWP should concentrate on defending the right of women to use cosmetics.

Another reader argued, "Of course these standards are bourgeois standards, but they are the norms the women have to meet. . . . If the women want these things, they should have them, and we have to support them. . . . It is part of the struggle of the women to emancipate themselves from the status of household drudges and to acquire an individuality of their own."

Political implications of differences

In order to organize the debate and let it unfold further, the Political Committee of the Socialist Workers Party, in October 1954, published a *Discussion Bulletin* containing other letters and articles that had been submitted, along with major replies by Evelyn Reed and Joseph Hansen, again using the name Jack Bustelo. The full scope of the reactionary pressure of that period is even clearer in some of this material, such as the article submitted by Marjorie McGowan, a member of the party's Los Angeles branch.

McGowan extolled "the revolution in technology and science" that, according to her, had "reached its highest development under capitalism in the last forty years" and had "wrought a partial revolution in all phases of life." This, she argued, had occurred "in the relation between the sexes, in sexual morality, in medicine, in nutrition and health, in architecture, in art, in beauty, in hobbies for leisure, in city planning, in child rearing, in methods of education, in psychology. . . ."

"These new, progressive, and highly creative developments in all phases of life," she continued, as if for the record, can only finally be realized by socialism. In the meantime, however, this "revolution" is changing everything for the better. That, she argued, is the proper context for the discussion on the marketing and use of cosmetics, because "what holds true for the rest of life also relates to beauty in the female form. . . ."

The revolutionary changes "in the standards of beauty," McGowan stated, "flow out of and parallel the concurrent revolution in sexual morality of the last thirty-five years or so. The long-stemmed American beauty," she raved on, "full of natural vitality and physical grace, with shining hair, clear eyes, smooth skin, and natural cosmetics with a trace of accent here and there, is no fiction but an American commonplace. This type of beauty is the

American social standard. . . ."

"It is an inherent part of every normal female ego to strive toward the preservation" of this kind of beauty, she argued, and "this is a proper female goal worthy of the considered attention of a revolutionist."

McGowan contemptuously eliminated any ambiguity about the class she looked to for leadership of the "revolution" whose praises she sang: "There is nothing beautiful in the dishpan hands, the premature wrinkles, the scraggly hair, the dumpy figures in the dumpy housedresses, the ugly furniture, and the hodge-podge accessories of the working-class woman and her home."

Not surprisingly, McGowan left the SWP a short time later.

Materialism abandoned

McGowan's espousal of the racist standards of "beauty" of the U.S. imperialist bourgeoisie, and her contempt for working-class women, were accompanied by an open rejection of the historical discoveries of materialists concerning the origin of women's oppression.

The Spring 1954 issue of the magazine *Fourth International,* also edited by Joseph Hansen, included an article by Evelyn Reed entitled "The Myth of Women's Inferiority." This was followed by the publication of "Sex and Labor in Primitive Society" by Reed in the Summer 1954 issue of the magazine. Both articles dealt with the evolution of human society through definite stages of economic and social development and explained that primitive communism, which was matriarchal in kinship structure, came first in this historical sequence.[3]

McGowan submitted a long article for the SWP *Discussion Bulletin* attempting to refute the positions expressed by Reed, which, McGowan said, were "scholastically irresponsible" and made the SWP "look ridiculous in the

eyes of informed individuals in the bourgeois academic world." McGowan demanded that the editors of *Fourth International* magazine and the SWP leadership repudiate these views.

In a cover letter addressed to the Political Committee, McGowan made it clear that she knew that her argument was with Karl Marx and Frederick Engels, not just with Evelyn Reed. She stated her "firm inner conviction that such interpretations of primitive society and primitive social forms as are current in the party today, and have been for the last seventy-five years or so, are not just accidentally false or innocently misguided."

As Reed noted in her reply, "I know of only one interpretation of primitive society which has been current in the party for the last seventy-five years or so, and which, indeed, we have openly embraced. This is the *Marxist* interpretation, as it was set down by Engels in his *Origin of the Family, Private Property and the State.*"

The Political Committee rejected McGowan's request that the magazine's editors dissociate themselves from Reed's positions.

"The Political Committee felt it unnecessary to take a position either for or against Comrade Reed's articles," SWP National Secretary Farrell Dobbs wrote in an October 13, 1954, letter to McGowan. "On such subjects the feeling was that considerable latitude is permissible so long as the author defends the materialist viewpoint, advocates and tries to apply the dialectic method, and seeks to supply material of an educational character. . . . From this standpoint, the editors were entirely correct in publishing the Reed articles."

McGowan's criticism of Reed, as well as Reed's reply, are reproduced in the final section of this book. Although dated, these pieces remain of interest today because they present the two fundamentally counterposed schools of thought in the great "hundred-year debate" on the origins of class-divided society and women's oppression.

As with the rest of the material published here, no attempt has been made to edit this exchange in light of later information or clarification. It is sufficient to note that throughout the subsequent twenty-five years of her life, Reed continued her research, kept abreast of new developments in the field, and published extensively on all the questions touched on in this exchange with McGowan on historical materialism and the origins of women's oppression. She never returned to this particular piece to correct errors or prepare it for broader circulation.

A movement of opposition, not adaptation

Both Reed and Hansen (still using the pen name of Bustelo) also wrote major articles for the *Discussion Bulletin* taking up the issues raised directly by the "cosmetics" debate. The polemical tone and language of their contributions reflect their origin and purpose, which was to advance political clarification within the SWP. No attempt has been made to change the authors' original styles. Readers will find in these pages all the rich flavor of a real debate, the product of the political conditions and social pressures of the time.

Bustelo's article, entitled "The Fetish of Cosmetics," is a basic piece of Marxist education on capitalism and commodity fetishism. It explains the controversy in the context of the economic and social conditions of post-World War II U.S. society. The author's sense of humor, moreover, makes for enjoyable reading.

Reed's reply, "The Woman Question and the Marxist Method," takes up the issues from a materialist standpoint, as well: norms of beauty, like humanity itself, are the historical and changing product of social labor and cannot be dissociated from the development of the productive forces or from the class struggle.

Reed also comments on the social and political context

of the debate. The "past fourteen years of war boom and prosperity have produced a conservatizing effect upon the working class which we describe as a 'bourgeoisification,'" she states. "One of the forms this takes is the readiness of the workers to accept bourgeois opinions and propaganda as scientific truth and adapt themselves to it.

"Like the whole working class," Reed emphasized, "the party is under constant pressure and bombardment from this massive bourgeois propaganda machine." Some of the discussions taking place in the SWP indicate that "a certain amount of adaptation to bourgeois propaganda has arisen which, although probably unwitting, is a signal that should alert us to the danger."

That is what the cosmetics controversy clearly revealed. "When the comrades defend the *right* of women to use cosmetics, fashions, etc.," Reed stated, "without clearly distinguishing between such a right and the capitalist *social compulsion* to use them, they have fallen into the trap of bourgeois propaganda."

It is true, she went on, that "so long as capitalism prevails, we must abide by these cosmetic and fashion decrees. . . . We must give at least a token recognition of the harsh reality. But this does not mean that we must accept these edicts and compulsions complacently, or without protest. The workers in the plants are often obliged to accept speedups, pay cuts, and attacks on their unions. But they always and invariably accept them under protest, under continuing struggle against them, and in a constant movement to *oppose* their needs and will against their exploiters.

"The class struggle is a movement of *opposition*, not *adaptation*," Reed said, "and this holds true not only of the workers in the plants, but of the women as well. . . ."

That conclusion, we could add, holds equally true for today. And in that spirit, the following book has been prepared.

NOVEMBER 1985

EDITOR'S NOTE

The article "Sagging Cosmetic Lines Try a Face Lift" by Jack Bustelo (Joseph Hansen), and the exchange of letters to the editor commenting on it, originally appeared in the July 26–September 6, 1954, issues of the U.S. socialist news-weekly, the *Militant*. All the other contents are reprinted from an October 1954 issue of the Socialist Workers Party's *Discussion Bulletin*.

These materials have been edited to correct obvious typographical errors and to introduce stylistic consistency. The citations are the responsibility of the original authors. Notes and an index have been supplied by the editor. A substantially shortened and edited version of Evelyn Reed's article on cosmetics originally appeared in *Problems of Women's Liberation* also published by Pathfinder Press.

Sonja Franeta

1. From the pages of the 'Militant'

"A Skin You Love to Touch"

By Henry Hutt

This cover of a Jergens Lotion advertising brochure provided the slogan "a skin you love to touch."

Jack Bustelo

Sagging cosmetic lines
try a face lift

Have you noticed lately that there are fewer girls around with skins you love to touch?[4]

It's not something the matter with your eyes. It's really so. The Toilet Goods Association reports that after thirteen years of steady gains, cosmetics manufacturers' sales suddenly plunged in the first quarter of 1954—right when unemployment took a steep jump. The figures haven't been revealed, but they must have been startling, for the unexpected decline in the use of lipstick, face cream, rouge, powder, eyebrow paint, hair set, fingernail enamel, and pimple killers sent a scare through the industry.

However, don't get alarmed. The school-girl complexion, unlike the cigar-store Indian, is not yet on the way out. Gallant champions are rushing to the scene of danger, prepared to give their all for a great American institution.

To save the $1,000,000,000 a year market, and perhaps win the biggest share of it at the same time, three manufacturers alone, Hazel Bishop, Incorporated, Revlon Products

Corporation, and the Toni Division of Gillette Company, are dumping more than $33,000,000 into ad programs for their products this next calendar year. And that, according to the July 16 *Wall Street Journal,* which is breathless with the news, is an estimated 30 percent over last year.

Other champions of beauty are equally eager for the honor and profit of rescuing American womanhood from dishpan hands, oily skin, stringy hair, telltale flakes, wrinkled necks, and double chins. The list includes Warner-Hudnut, Inc., Lehn & Fink, Procter & Gamble, Helena Rubenstein, Helene Curtis Industries, Harriet Hubbard Ayer, and Elizabeth Arden.

Operation Big Push

Operation Big Push among these competitors is being readied right now for next month. Already a few beachheads have been taken. Toni, for example, has announced its third new cosmetic in three months, a face cream that no words can describe except Deep Magic. That follows a shampoo, christened Pamper, and a sockeroo in lipsticks, Viv.

A cool $5,000,000 has been earmarked to blast these over radio and TV, the aim being to pound into the head of every girl and woman in the land the fundamental principle of the cosmetics industry; namely, that good complexions, fair hands, and lovely hair are not born, they're made.

Revlon, too, has entered the fray, banners flying. Lanolite lipstick is their battle cry, two tints, one for morning and one for evening. And to keep your hair just where it should be on that moonlit beach, air-bomb your head with Silken Net.

Hazel Bishop, not to be mouse-trapped, has a liquid rouge, Complexion Glo, to put the right color in your cheeks. And the company announced secret weapons, soon to be unveiled, for reprisal against Max Factor's Cream Puff and Pond Extract's Angel Face.

'Chameleonlike'

Hudnut's new products include Quick, a home permanent that will crimp your hair in nothing flat; Hair Repair for use if something goes wrong or you get bleached out in wind, sun, sand, or rain; and Bloom, a rouge so out of this world it can only be described as having a "chameleonlike quality."

Procter & Gamble, one of the high and mighty in the kingdom of soap, is punching into the cosmetics fight with Lilt, a home permanent. And against Toni's pincurl wave, Bobbi, it is giving test runs on Pin-It for range, speed, and fire power.

On the unwanted hair front there's exciting news. Arden is already opening up a barrage on TV for its new hair-removing cream, Sleek, which helps you keep up that sheer and lovely look by keeping down ugly stubble and five o'clock shadow.

In the nail enamel sector of the battle for beauty, Revlon holds the lead at present, but others promise fierce competition. Revlon's big reserve battery is a list of 7,000 hues. Twice a year it picks out a new tint and spreads it from coast to coast on millions of fingertips and toes under such delectable names as "Fire and Ice" or "Kissing Pink."

Queen Bee Cream

In face creams, General Beauty Products Corporation, a subsidiary of Coty, has come up with what promises to be a blockbuster, if not an atom bomb: Queen Bee Cream, a cream based on the substance bees feed selected larvae in the hive to make them become queens. It's especially designed for girls with that wormlike feeling.

In the struggle to save the American girl from lapsing back into the barbaric customs of the past, when soap and water gave a complexion that clean look on weekdays, and a touch of strawberry juice and rice powder that extra finish needed at the Saturday night dance, the cosmetics manufacturers have mobilized some of the country's top advertising generals.

Put over Serutan

One of the most dreaded by other manufacturers is Hazel Bishop's ad expert, Mr. Spector. He was the one who took a simple but surefire laxative and made it a nationwide habit by merely spelling "natures" backward. Since 1950 he has lifted Hazel Bishop from a debt-ridden status to sales of $11,000,000 last year and a projected $18,000,000 for this year.

Against him are ranged such figures as R.N. and Irving Harris who developed a home permanent-wave kit in 1944 and in four years built it into a $20,000,000 a year business with the aid of such dazzling slogans as "Which Twin Has the Toni?"

With brains like that working on the problem, with all that competitive interest, and with all those millions pouring into advertising channels, I think we can all feel safe— well at least half-safe. They'll convince America's women to stay beautiful.

Please, girls, don't let a cutback on the job mean a cutback on cosmetics. If you take a layoff, don't lay off the lipstick. Remember, to keep up prosperity, keep up your makeup.

Cosmetics and the women

Editor:

I would like to make some criticisms of the article entitled "Sagging Cosmetic Lines Try a Face Lift" in the July 26 issue.

I am not taking issue with the intention of the author as it is apparent that he means to hit the cosmetics companies, which make a business of exploiting the deep yearnings of women for their own greater profits. In spite of the obvious purpose of the article, however, one gets the feeling that it is the women who are being made fun of.

In order to effectively attack these companies, we have to first understand why women are so vulnerable to their advertising schemes. Rather than presenting women as being a little ridiculous, we have to know what they want, sympathize with them, and then translate their desires into action by showing that they can get all these things only through socialism.

Now what is it that women want, which makes it easy for

the cosmetics companies to wring out of these strivings profits for themselves? They want some loveliness and beauty in their lives. They want to rise above the sweaty grind of the shop, which distorts their bodies, and breaks down their spirit with fatigue and hopelessness. The housewife wants to break away from the monotony and dull routine of trying to manage on a worker's wages. Not only is she bogged down with innumerable chores, so that she has no time to take care of herself, but she can't afford good clothes. Soon all the youth and attractiveness, which by right belong to her, are snatched away, and both wife and husband are left with a feeling that they have been robbed of something essential.

We have to recognize that like many of the other good things in life, such as leisure to study, travel, appreciation of art and literature, beauty is predominantly monopolized by the wealthy. Whatever beauty a woman has in her early years, if she has been lucky enough to have had some advantages during childhood, is quickly dissipated among the working class. If she has to struggle against all odds to maintain her health, what chance has she to maintain her attractiveness?

The wealthy are beautiful because the workers are wretched. If we understand that, we can show the women a way out of this dilemma. This striving has a progressive aspect because it is part of the rebellion of women against a position which denies to them part of their rights as human beings.

On the basis of the havoc caused by capitalism and the confusion among the women, these cosmetics companies are then able to perpetrate a fraud and an outrage against these women. They promise to give to them what capitalism has taken away. We can show that socialism will bring to flower beauty in all its forms, and that every individual will be developed to his fullest capacity, both physically and intellectually.

Louise Manning
LOS ANGELES, CALIFORNIA

Is beauty deeper than cosmetics?

Editor:

I appreciate Louise Manning's criticism in last week's *Militant* of my article "Sagging Cosmetic Lines Try a Face Lift." She raises some interesting and important questions that go beyond what was intended in my report in the July 26 issue of the declining cosmetics sales and what the hucksters plan to do about it.

On one point, however, I must disagree with her. I do not believe that "beauty is predominantly monopolized by the wealthy" and that the "wealthy are beautiful because the workers are wretched."

It appears to me that you might just as well say that "morality is predominantly monopolized by the wealthy," and that the "wealthy are moral because the workers are immoral."

If you were to try to prove that the wealthy are beautiful by citing examples, certain difficulties would at once arise. Among the bourgeoisie, what period would you choose? The period of their rise, when the closefisted miser and the puritanical house economist were the models? Or the period of imperialist expansion, when the pigeon-breasted officer strutting his war ribbons and medals is the model? Or a period of ostentatious wealth when the stockholder lounging on a yacht deck is the model? Clearly, it is difficult to find absolute beauty within bourgeois society. The ideal seems to change.

Seeking a firmer standard, we might go beyond the limits of capitalist society and compare its concepts of beauty with that of other societies. For example, the postwar American bourgeois ideal of the beautiful bosom—the upholstered, steel-girdered front (or the flattened chest recently decreed by Christian Dior to replace it)—would make an interesting subject for comparative study with say the Balinese ideal where women prefer their breasts free of clothing.

In the field of cosmetics we might compare the frozen mask of the neurosis-ridden bourgeois clotheshorse with the primitive who beautifies himself by filing his teeth, putting a bone in his nose, saucers in his ear lobes, and who makes his hair alluring with rancid butter. And, really, is the one more beautiful than the other?

Even in feet, it is difficult to find an absolute standard transcending society. The current bourgeois ideal of beauty there—a woman balanced on spiked heels—is perhaps better than the ideal of the rich Chinese mandarin whose wife, out of devotion to beauty, bound her feet. But then how do both compare with the sandal wearers? Or with those who go barefoot?

From a materialist point of view, the norms of beauty like the norms of morals, are functions of society. Although the relation may be remote, they are determined in the final analysis by the ruling class. The norms are far from fixed. And when a revolution comes along, they are often deposed with startling swiftness.

I think that when capitalist society gives way to socialism, and the new generations take stock of what they have inherited, not much in the bourgeois lumber room of morals and beauty will prove very useful.

The new society will at first probably be much more interested in truth, above all the truth about the human mind, its physical under-structure, its endowments, its relation to other minds, its potentialities and how to realize them.

From the study of such patterns in the world brotherhood of enduring peace and well-being will emerge—if I may venture a prediction—completely new and unsuspected fields where the great artists of the future will again consider the problem of beauty on a qualitatively different level.

The emphasis on cosmetics in our miserable, superficial society will then be seen for what it really is, one of the signs of the barbarism of the times. Lovers of beauty in the new society will feel no need, I believe, to decorate lilies.

As to the feeling that Louise Manning expresses of my presenting "women as being a little ridiculous" despite my good intentions, I am somewhat at a loss for an answer. I do not deny that the unconscious can play tricks on us, but I hope that I will be held responsible only for what I was aware of.

I think most of the customs and norms of capitalist society are ridiculous and even vicious, including the customs and norms of wealthy bourgeois women. As for so-called ordinary women, whether housewives or workers, I think they are beautiful, no matter how toil worn or seasoned in experience, for they are the ones who will be in the forefront of the struggle to build a new and better world.

They will be admired in future times the way we admire the hardy, ax-swinging pioneer women of America, for their beauty lies in their character and it is manifest not in the cosmetics they indulge in but the deeds they perform.

Jack Bustelo
NEW YORK CITY

Lives in world as it is today

Editor:

I too, along with Louise Manning, was a bit disturbed by the Jack Bustelo article on cosmetics. I happen to be a working woman with a family to look after. Thus I very much appreciated the article on the seventy-two-hour workweek of working mothers a few issues back.

Maybe the long hours in a factory with the job of housekeeping and child care after work has something to do with the fact that I don't have rosy cheeks but a good splattering of wrinkles and pimples instead. Maybe it has something to do with the fact that my eyes don't sparkle and that my legs are tired and that my feet hurt. Maybe you, Jack, want to laugh and ridicule my using popular cosmetics to overcome some of these difficulties of working for a living. Laugh if you want, but I doubt if even you would laugh if I told you I don't have the money to go to a doctor about my pimples nor do I have the time off work to rest up and get some sunshine into my cheeks at some lakeside resort.

Or maybe you really believe what you wrote in answer to Louise Manning that "ordinary women, whether housewives or workers . . . no matter how toil worn or seasoned in experience" are beautiful. If you do, then I see why you ridicule our efforts to appear a little less bruised and tired than we really are. But for me, I live in the world as it is today, with its standards of beauty and its social customs. It means a good deal to me that my husband, my children, my shop mates, and my friends enjoy my company and that I can contribute something to the beauty and joy of our association today according to today's standards and not the standards of the future society.

In this world of mine, the woman factory worker's world, it is fairly common knowledge that "beauty is predominantly monopolized by the wealthy." I for one, and I think I could speak for all the girls in the shop I work in, would like very much to have some of the beautiful clothes that you see hanging on a "bourgeois clotheshorse." We would also like to have taken the vacation trip the boss's wife just got back from. Say, did she have a beautiful tan and a sparkle in her eyes when she got back!

Maybe you think we girls are mistakenly desirous of indulging in some "ridiculous and even vicious" capitalist norms? Think again, Jack, Louise Manning is absolutely correct when she views our desires and struggles as "part of the rebellion against a position which denies to them their rights as human beings." Your article on cosmetics was not too bad taken as a whole, but brother, you sure put your foot in it when you attempted an answer to Louise Manning's criticism.

F.J.
"SEASONED AND EXPERIENCED"
GARMENT WORKER
SAN FRANCISCO, CALIFORNIA

Cosmetics and economic pressure

Editor:

In an article on the cosmetics industry a few weeks ago, you poked fun, expertly, at the ridiculous advertisements of the companies, and facetiously advocated a return to pure soap, water, and berry juice for women. Personally, I would be greatly relieved if I could forego the trouble and expense of makeup, but capitalism won't let me. I'm no sucker for beauty-aid ads, but economic pressure—I have to earn my living—forces me to buy and use the darned stuff.

Cosmetics are a prize example of the special discrimination that women workers are subjected to. Far from being a luxury (and they are taxed as such), cosmetics are a grim necessity for the older or not physically blessed woman worker. She must constantly compete, in the labor market and on the job, against younger or more attractive girls. The male boss who selects experienced and efficient workers, rather than those who radiate a Hollywood-like glamor, is rare indeed.

A qualified male worker applying for a job is acceptable,

socially, as long as he is normally clean and neat. And soiled jeans and a day-old growth of beard are considered "normal"—for a man. But the woman applicant must be not only qualified technically, she must be well dressed, groomed to the teeth, every hair in place, and exuding charm. If the seams in her hose are twisted, that's evidence of carelessness of details. If she wears no makeup, she's obviously peculiar or neurotic or both; if she wears too much, she's a hussy; and if she looks worried (which she usually is—over her appearance!), she's completely unacceptable because "tense women make the boss nervous."

When she comes home after a hard day at work, she usually puts in eight more hours cooking, cleaning, tending to the children, etc. But there's still no rest for her—along about midnight, she's exhaustedly putting up her hair, tweezing her brows, and fussing with creams that just might dissolve wrinkles, so that the boss won't know she lied about her age to get the job. And then comes the inevitable, horrible moment when she has to decide what in the hell to wear the next day or—how to make three outfits appear like six.

Almost *every* employment agency has different application blanks for men and women; on the latter, there is a special section with blanks after a list of words like "Appearance," "Complexion," "Personality," "Speech," and "Grooming." But despite all the preparation necessary to get and hold a job compared to the time, energy, and thought a man has to devote to this question, the woman still continues to receive less pay for equal work on too many jobs.

But here's the payoff on the importance placed on cosmetics today. If a wife strays from the paths of marital fidelity, the irate husband is firmly advised—by Inez Robb of the Hearst Press—to give the female sinner a firm paddling. He can even shoot her and get sympathy from a jury. But if a husband strays from a worn-out housewife with boisterous children, a broken-down washing machine, mountains of clothes to be mended, and a discouraged sag in her shoulders, the columnists all holler that it's all her own fault for not having changed her hairstyle and applied lipstick every morning!

So I'm afraid I'll have to stick to Max Factor's Pancake instead of rice powder—until such time as present-day standards of sex beauty as a requisite for getting a job are thrown onto the rubbish heap along with the rest of the artificial standards of the capitalist system.

Helen Baker
SEATTLE, WASHINGTON

The ruling class's
standards of beauty

Editor:

In my humble opinion the letter by Louise Manning headed "Cosmetics and the Women" misses the pertinent points in relation to women, beauty, cosmetics, and socialism.

I use cosmetics, but I know that in doing so I am simply making a concession to the standards of capitalist society. Under this society women (and men) are to some extent ridiculous: they are ridiculous from the standards which will exist under socialism, and are already held to a limited extent by those of us who struggle for it. To the supporters of capitalism or of its standards of beauty, cosmetics do increase feminine beauty; but in previous societies women have stretched their ears and lips, pierced their noses, and restricted their feet, and to the supporters of those societies that was beautiful. It does not seem beautiful to us now because we do not have the beauty standards of those barbaric societies.

When Louise Manning writes, "The wealthy are beautiful because the workers are wretched," she reveals that her standard of beauty is derived from capitalist society. The wealthy are beautiful only by their own standards which in the long run assign women the roles of mother and plaything. For this, youth is considered paramount. Bourgeois women accordingly seek to give the appearance of youth with the aid of cosmetics, inflatable bras, face lifting, etc. Capitalist standards of feminine beauty are established primarily by men who, corrupted by an exploiting society, cannot see women as anything more than mothers and playthings. That a woman might be a fully developed human being, capable of much that cannot be achieved in bed, never occurs to the undisguised ideologists of capitalism.

The Marxist standard of beauty, like Marxist morality, is taken from the needs of the struggle to bring socialism into the world. That struggle requires intelligence, courage, intellectual honesty, compassion, and a firm will, among other things. Without benefit of cosmetics a face can indicate one or more of these qualities even through a network of wrinkles, and thus achieve beauty. A face can be ever so smooth, ever so cleverly painted to a simulation of youthful bloom, but indicate, truly or falsely, narrowness of outlook, cupidity, cowardice, or moral weakness, and thus be revoltingly ugly.

Women's present adherence to bourgeois society is indicated, in fact, by their devotion to the standards of beauty of the ruling class. In this they are ridiculous, and not "progressive," not "rebellious" as Louise Manning would have us think. But the working-class women, like the working class generally, are abandoning these bourgeois standards. There will be some feminine picket lines and barricades in the future which, if not manned by Miss Universes, will nevertheless achieve real beauty in the militancy, intelligence, and social understanding developed by the combatants.

E. Patrick
LOS ANGELES, CALIFORNIA

We have to know what
women want

Editor:

The beginnings of a discussion do not always indicate differences which later develop in a more precise form. Jack Bustelo in his article on cosmetics and in his answer to Louise Manning now shows more clearly what the problem is.

In our approach to the women, we have to avoid sectarianism just as we do in any other field of our activity. It would be well not to fall into the same trap as the "third period" Stalinists,[5] when their sectarianism led them to scoff at the existing standards and made them the object of ridicule by the masses.

It is a serious mistake to counterpose our own standards of what is attractive to the demands of the masses of women. We are not discussing what these standards were in primitive society, or what they will be under socialism, or what we think they should be now. As a revolutionary party, we have to know what the women want today, since these desires stem from standards which they have to meet constantly in all their activities. We cannot bypass these by saying they are not important, and that we should look for more permanent values in the personality of the women.

The women want good clothes. They want to go to the beauty parlor for permanents and haircuts. They need time and money for these things. The concept that a woman should be satisfied with ill-fitting, poor quality clothing, or that her hair and makeup do not matter because there are more important things, is fostered by the wealthy, not for their own consumption, but to make the working-class woman bear her lot more cheerfully. We have to cut through all that. Of course these standards are bourgeois standards, but they are the norms the women have to meet. No one knows yet what standards under socialism will be. What right do we have to say to the women, "All these things which the wealthy have are not necessary for you"?

If the women want these things, they should have them, and we have to support them in their struggle to get them. This struggle is more than just a superficial fight to look better. It is part of the struggle of the women to emancipate themselves from the status of household drudges, and to acquire an individuality of their own.

Society is wealthy enough to grant these material factors to the women, but they will have to conduct a revolutionary struggle to get them. Afterwards, under socialism, when new needs and new desires arise, they may discard what they are seeking today, but let us not substitute the society of the future for the needs of today.

Sam Stern
LOS ANGELES, CALIFORNIA

2. The discussion in the SWP

Letter on Bustelo article

Editors:

I wish to enter the discussion in the paper on the subject of cosmetics with the blunt statement that I found Jack Bustelo's article "Sagging Cosmetic Lines Try a Face Lift" both offensive and presumptuous in tone, and false in content and implications. I believe that the editors should exercise more discrimination in the publication of articles concerning which there may be controversy—or quite possibly what is indicated is a controversy which will clear up for the editors in what way they should be discriminating. At any rate, it seemed clear to this reader that the Bustelo article was sharply out of place in the paper with its high standards of revolutionary journalism. Bustelo's subsequent letter of August 16, a fabric of half-truths laid out in a pattern of fancy but meaningless prose, only carried to its logical conclusion the implications and undertones of the first article, and for this reason I wish to deal with the letter rather than the offending article.

His entire August 16 letter is rooted in an erroneous assumption: that the revolution will create, out of the whole cloth, entire new standards of morality and beauty, and that "not much in the lumber room of bourgeois morals and beauty will prove very useful." I believe this to be both false and unscientific.

The revolution in technology and science, which reached its highest development under capitalism in the last forty years or so, has wrought a partial revolution in all phases of life—in the relation between the sexes, in sexual morality, in medicine, in nutrition and health, in architecture, in art, in beauty, in hobbies for leisure, in city planning, in child rearing, in methods of education, in psychology—a revolution in life and in living which cannot be completed and consummated until released from the restrictions and bonds imposed by the private ownership in the means of production. These new, progressive, and highly creative developments in all phases of life stand in sharp opposition to and are caught up in dynamic contradiction with the antiquated economic system of capitalism. They cannot be deepened and extended throughout the entire social body and find their expression as the new and modern way of life until freed by the world-wide socialist revolution. Only then can the new and revolutionary development expand unhindered throughout the world.

It is unscientific to conceive, as does Bustelo, that socialism will throw out everything which it inherits from capitalism and create everything new starting from the beginning. Rather, socialism will keep all that is revolutionary and progressive and all that men and women by their demands and desires wish to keep as good and worthy of further development. In my opinion, there will be a vast indebtedness which the socialist world will, in hindsight, accredit to capitalism, including much of its "lumber room of morals and beauty."

Socialism, for instance, will not throw out the morality of bourgeois society in toto and create a new one out of the whole cloth. Morality has been in the process of evolution during all of the centuries of mankind and the socialist society is not going to write off a part of the historical heritage of the human race as being totally useless. Rather, socialism will extract the hypocrisy and the mysticism out of bourgeois morality and leave the universal ideals of human brotherhood and make a reality of the Golden Rule.

Nor will socialism throw out the revolution which is taking place in modern architecture, with its unity of the natural and the man-made; nor the trend toward the decentralization and planning of cities going on before our eyes in the creation of tracts with their schools, stores, and social services—anarchistic, to be sure, at the hands of the builders and realtors. Rather, socialism will free this revolution from the bonds of the profit system, and cities will be planned for the use, convenience, and beauty of living, rather than for the profit of the realtors, speculators, and contractors.

Nor can we conceive of socialism rejecting the revolution which is taking place in art. Art has pervaded all phases of life. Pots, pans, fabrics, furniture, lamps, stoves, landscaping, architecture—*all* objects in the environment have become mediums for the creative expression of the artist and the designer. Art is no longer restricted to formalistic classifications, as sculpture or pictures hung on the walls of the wealthy or in museums, but is diffused and coordinated in the beauty and the unity of all objects in the environment of the wealthy, the upper middle class, and even in the homes of some of the more privileged workers. Socialist man is not going to dismiss these manifestations of new and vitally progressive art forms, starting all over with something new and different and inconceivable to our minds because unknown and unrelated to its past development. Rather, the revolution in art forms will no longer be just for those who can afford them, or be shackled with mortgages and time-payments, but will be the rightful heritage of every citizen in the communal world. Communist man will make an art of his way of life, surrounding himself with the creative outpourings of his inherent talent.

Nor will the socialist world create entire new forms of occupation for leisure hours out of the whole cloth. As an example, Comrade Cannon's theory of the resurgence of handicrafts is taking place on all social levels in the tremendous boom in the do-it-yourself crafts. The revolution will complete and free this trend which clearly expresses and fulfills a driving need in man, and will make it economically possible to have both the leisure and the material means to engage in craft activities.

These are only a few examples of what is meant by the revolution in living. We could go on with further illustrations, but suffice it to say that socialism will not create entire new standards in medicine, health, nutrition, child rearing, psychology, methods of teaching, etc., unrelated from their historic past and their present development. Instead, it will extend and continue the revolution which capitalist technology has already commenced, but freed from the contradictions and restrictions imposed by a decadent, reactionary political-economic system.

What holds true for the rest of life also relates to beauty in the female form around which the discussion on cosmetics revolves. The development of the future must be sought out in the seeds of the present. The beauty of tomorrow will not be created out of nothing but out of the living forces and tendencies of today. This is the only scientific way to proceed in any question; we do not engage in a star-gazing or crystal-ball divining. Jack Bustelo, however, didn't look at what 40 or 50 million women want today as a basis for deciding what they might want in the future. Rather, in pompous disregard for the aspirations of modern women, he rejects these aspirations as false and depicts the women as mere ignorant dupes of the capitalist hucksters.

I personally find it inexcusable that column space should be given to a self-appointed judge of what constitutes feminine strivings and what constitutes a social norm of female beauty all under the pretext of a survey of one phase of the American economy. I wholeheartedly endorse the right of self-determination in the very personal matter of what strikes the individual as beautiful, but *social* norms of beauty are determined *socially*, not by the dictates of some individual or other. Bustelo has a right to his own opinion of what he considers beautiful. However, involved here is not his opinion per se, but the fact that he has set up his opinion against the strivings of millions of women in capitalist society and said, in effect: "The well-scrubbed look shall be the standard of tomorrow and should be the standard of today. Let us not gild the lily. I see all this in my crystal ball."

Not only does he show a remarkable ignorance of female psychology, but as remarkable an ignorance of the history and meaning of cosmetics. As he points out with considerable flourish, the mores in beauty change, evolve, and grow along with developing civilization. However, all of this change and the course of its development cannot be reduced to one source as he attempts to do—to the dictates of a ruling class in a class society. However the mores might change, the strivings for beauty are the product of profoundly powerful forces implicit in the human personality and in the relation between the sexes, and have a more direct relation to the forces of reproduction than to those of production. The use of cosmetics and other means of bodily decoration are older than written history and women were gilding the lily long before the class struggle came into existence, and from all the signposts of today, they shall continue to do so long after the class struggle has passed out of existence. As such, this is a question which both transcends the confines of the class relationships, and, at the same time, is contained and determined by it.

The fact is, as in all other phases of life in capitalist America, a revolution has been going on in standards of beauty side by side with and flowing out of the revolution in technology. This revolution is more than cosmetic-deep. It involves the glow of physical health and good nutrition which stands in direct relation to the higher standards of living of the American economy. It also involves the freer and more informal mode of attire, the more natural gestures and grace of movement, which flow out of and parallel the concurrent revolution in sexual morality of the last thirty-five years or so. The long-stemmed American beauty, full of natural vitality and physical grace, with shining hair, clear eyes, smooth skin, and natural cosmetics with a trace of accent here and there, is no fiction but an American commonplace. This type of beauty is the American social standard, whatever Bustelo might think of it, but by and large it is the exclusive property of first of all youth, and secondly of wealth. If this American beauty is also neurosis-ridden, as our observant Bustelo comments upon, this only demonstrates that things are considerably more complicated than they seem. But why throw out the baby with the bath?

The cosmetics industry and their hucksters do not thrive on the natural beauty which is the birthright of youth of whatever class. It thrives on the lilies who have begun to fade, a phenomenon of nature which strikes every woman in her thirties. And in days of yesteryear, a woman was rated old by the time she reached her forties. It is an inherent part of every normal female ego to strive toward the preservation of youthful beauty, and this is a proper female goal worthy of the considered attention of a revolutionist. The goal of preserving youth as long as reasonably possible has always occupied the attention of the human race, but for the woman of the working class to achieve this goal, considerable effort and expense is entailed. Once the fresh bloom of youth is gone, the working-class woman has neither the means to patronize the beauty shops nor the energy after wrestling with pots, pans, and children to devote to the preservation of personal beauty, and soon she has joined the ranks of the drab millions, cheated of a good part of life's thrill. But one look at the radiance of movie stars in their middle forties, achieved solely through a higher standard of living and the alchemy of the modern beauty temples, is enough to convince millions of women that this is something they want too. Who, we may ask, is Jack Bustelo to leave us with the implication that this is something ridiculous? And who is he to set himself up as a self-styled authority on the merits of soap and water (not to speak of rice powder!) as opposed to all the women who find that creams and lotions do a better job? And who is he to say that the quest for personal beauty is not a legitimate goal of all women; that character is more the ticket?

This finding of beauty in the spirit and character of the working-class woman is legitimate for a revolutionist. But let us not confuse the means and ends. There is nothing beautiful in the dishpan hands, the premature wrinkles, the scraggly hair, the dumpy figures in dumpy housedresses, the ugly furniture, and the hodge-podge accessories of the working-class woman and her home. To find beauty there is nothing other than the ultra-leftism of the radical snob— an affectation—belonging to the days when long hair and dirty ears were the hallmark of the real honest-to-goodness radical. If the hungry spirit of the working-class woman did not yearn for the beautiful surroundings which are the exclusive property of the leisure and upper middle class; if the women did not hunger for personal beauty in their bodies, in their clothes, in their environment, there wouldn't be any struggle, nor any revolution, nor any socialism. The spirit is, indeed, a beautiful thing because it is alive, vital, and progressive. But the spirit moves out and away from the dirt, squalor, and the grind of today toward the beauty of the free world of tomorrow. He who finds magnificence in squalor, or even satisfaction in it, will never rise above it. But he or she whom the spirit moves shall find at the end of the struggle the true goals of the human race.

Marjorie McGowan
LOS ANGELES, CALIFORNIA

More on cosmetics

Jack Bustelo's article on cosmetics and his letter entitled "Is Beauty Deeper Than Cosmetics?" make the point that the beauty of working-class women, like the beauty of the pioneer woman "lies in their character and it is manifest not in the cosmetics they indulge in but the deeds they perform."

Let me say, first of all, that working-class women do not "indulge in" cosmetics. Our use of cosmetics is far from an indulgence—it is basically an economic necessity and from this has become an aesthetic necessity.

If a woman applying for office work, a waitress job, or domestic work forgets about her personal appearance and ignores it, she will surely be the last to be hired, unless she has some really exceptional skill or background.

In unskilled factory work the appearance of physical strength and stamina counts the most. But even in this case, the appearance of stamina, youth, and vigor is augmented by cosmetics. You can't go out hunting even a factory job, looking as tired as you might feel—cosmetics brighten up a weary face and give the illusion of the necessary vigor and youth.

Do you know, Mr. Bustelo, that a young woman who has only minor office skills is already a glut on the labor market at the age of twenty-five? Employers advertising for office help will very often indicate that "under twenty-five" is all they are considering. Youthfulness is admired by the employer not for aesthetic reasons at all, as one might imagine, but merely because it indicates a greater capacity for energetic work. Do you disapprove if women "indulge in cosmetics" to acquire the bright-eyed, youthful, healthy, and vigorous look needed to get such jobs?

But all women cannot work and support themselves. Jobs are not as plentiful for women as for men. Those jobs which are open to women pay a great deal less. And this simple economic fact creates the great competitive enterprise known as "getting and keeping a husband." (One would think that men would recognize this and fight for equal job rights for women, if only to free themselves of the compulsive element in marriage.)

This grandiose competition, which has countless forms, both open and subtle, consumes a great part of women's time and thought. And one of the major tools of this competition is sexual accentuation through the use of cosmetics.

Although this is often viewed as more of "women's trickery," it is not something to be laid at their doorstep. At bottom it is an economic problem. Capitalism cannot provide jobs for all the members of the working class—male and female. The male half of the population is expected to support the female half—marriage is the medium for this—and the most complex, fantastic, and subtle attitudes of morality and aesthetics are developed to help bring this male-female relationship into operation. (And by the way, this relationship which was once taken for granted, breaks down in the decline of capitalism and forces many married women to take on the double burden of domestic service in her home and wage work in the outside world.)

Accentuation of sexuality through cosmetics is necessary in the competition for a husband and economic security. This may be unfortunate or ridiculous or degrading, but it is also a bare fact of contemporary existence, stripped of all its romantic trimmings.

Mr. Bustelo may laugh at cosmetic "improvement" and sexual accentuation and ridicule the women victims who concentrate on this to the detriment of the rest of their personalities, but the capitalist system has conditioned him, and men in general, to respond to this kind of sexuality—often without even knowing what he is responding to.

However, it is true that if all the "ordinary women" had good health, a buoyant, optimistic attitude, well-made clothing, it would go a long way toward the destruction of the cosmetics industry. Good health, a good figure, a clear skin, sparkling eyes, lustrous hair—all these things come first of all from a good diet—not a starch-filled diet of too much bread and potatoes but a diet that includes plenty of eggs and steak and fresh vegetables. And a buoyant, optimistic attitude is the product of a happy life with perspectives for the future. Can capitalism give these things to all women?

Bustelo may be able to retain a warmth and affection toward the working-class woman who has had too little rest and too much anxiety and worry—he may admire her "moral beauty" but she herself and her husband and her friends will not find this consideration too useful. Very few people today can go along with Bustelo's attitude that "ordinary" women "are beautiful no matter how toil worn"—especially very few men. This moral beauty which is treasured by those who are more conscious than the average is not much use to the "ordinary" husband and wife whose aesthetic and sexual ideals are built on the "ordinary" standards.

Why shouldn't a woman paint her face, dye her hair, use

perfume and whatever else is necessary to help fulfill the aesthetic and sexual desires of both herself and her husband? Between Mr. Jack Bustelo and the world at large, she is damned if she does and damned if she doesn't.

It is quite true that the great use of cosmetics today is "one of the signs of the barbarism of the times," but not as Bustelo understands it. (Cosmetics are ancient, and have been used for many reasons, good and bad. They will probably be used even under socialism, by both men and women, for the pleasure of personal adornment.) The great use of cosmetics today is "a sign of barbarism" because it is *obligatory* and necessary. Because we do not always use cosmetics simply because we choose to do so. This is the barbarism, not the thing itself. And it is a sign of barbarism because it exposes the fact that the physical appearance of women is made to assume such a great and decisive importance in this society, and the other aspects of her personality are subordinated almost to the point of extinction. But I for one, want to have my cake and eat it too. I wish to improve and enjoy my physical appearance and at the same time improve and develop all the other sides of my personality. And I think all women have a *right* to both these things.

Why doesn't Mr. Bustelo advocate good wages, plenty of money to *meet the necessity* of cosmetics—or a good diet and high standard of living to *lessen the need* for cosmetics?

Don't offer us "moral beauty" or a new aesthetic standard as a solution for today's "ordinary woman" in today's everyday world. Let's look forward to socialism for that, when everyone can develop new cultural and aesthetic ideals.

The point is this, Mr. Bustelo: AS LONG AS THE WORLD DEMANDS COSMETIC IMPROVEMENT, either for economic or aesthetic reasons, WOMEN HAVE EVERY RIGHT TO WHATEVER MEANS ARE NECESSARY TO MEET THAT DEMAND. And to ridicule us for bowing to that demand is rather poor taste, and an example of that cheap humor which makes a butt out of an easy victim. This alone is unworthy of the pages of the paper.

However, in addition, your point of view contains a political error. We are not going to change the world by revolting against such a sideline issue as this—and that seems to be what your article would have us do. If working-class women boycotted all cosmetics I doubt very much if it would help build a labor party or lessen Jim Crow or halt the war drive.

Jeanne Morgan
LOS ANGELES, CALIFORNIA

Evelyn Reed

The woman question and the Marxist method

As we have frequently pointed out, the past fourteen years of war boom and prosperity have produced a conservatizing effect upon the working class which we describe as a "bourgeoisification." One of the forms this takes is the readiness of the workers to accept bourgeois opinions and propaganda as scientific truth and adapt themselves to it.

Like the whole working class, the party is under constant pressure and bombardment from this massive bourgeois propaganda machine. As the conscious vanguard, however, we must not permit ourselves to become influenced by it to the slightest degree. On the contrary, we must counter this mood in the working class through unremitting ideological struggle.

Certain discussions now taking place in the party reveal that a certain amount of adaptation to bourgeois propaganda has arisen which, although probably unwitting, is a signal that should alert us to the danger. These discussions revolve around a very important and highly complex subject, the woman question. Since many aspects of this question are still obscure, and all aspects are sensitive, it is all the more imperative that we begin such a discussion on the basis of utmost clarity and objectivity.

For some months an informal discussion has been going on among some comrades on the problem of "male chauvinism" as it relates to the party.[6] A few comrades have felt that the party itself is not free from this and that women comrades are seriously hindered and handicapped by it. However, this question would require a document by itself to deal with all the elements involved and to discuss it on a historical and scientific basis.

The discussion on the woman question as it now exists, has been opened up through two written criticisms as follows:

1. A criticism of Jack Bustelo's article in the paper exposing the hucksters and economic perspectives of the cosmetics sector of big business is centered around women and beauty.

2. Comrade McGowan's criticism of my last article in the magazine centering around women and anthropology.

At first glance these appear to be two entirely different topics; one is a daily question concerning modern women and cosmetics, the other is a scientific question concerning women and anthropology. The comrades supporting one criticism may even be opposed to the other. The fact is, however, there is a connection between them. They both reveal that on the daily level and scientific level, we have become influenced by the bourgeois propaganda machine. Such an influence can only lead to adaptation to bourgeois methodology unless it is countered by its opposite, the Marxist method. The time is at hand, therefore, for a fresh review of the Marxist method as it is concretely applied to this important woman question.

Cosmetics, beauty, and labor

The discussion which was unleashed by Jack Bustelo's article in the paper has shifted the axis of Bustelo's limited aim; namely, to expose the profiteers and hucksters in the cosmetics sector of big business, who get rich by exploiting the ignorance, oppression, and fashion regimentation of women.

The arguments against him center around the "needs and wants" of women in the realm of sexual beauty which Bustelo, it seems, does not understand. Let us then listen to the women themselves on what they need and want. After reading through the criticisms, however, I find two main propositions, both of them contradictory, which may be summed up as follows: "Women want what they do not want."

This is not intended as a joke. These contradictions are a reflection of a society torn by contradictions of all kinds. They reveal, moreover, that while we are in the forefront when it comes to challenging bourgeois propaganda on economic and political questions, we are lagging behind in exposing bourgeois propaganda on questions that concern women: sex, female beauty, the family, and so on. We have been leaving the field to the bourgeoisie and their propaganda machine, with the result that some comrades have swallowed some indigestible bait but don't quite know what it is.

The two contradictory propositions are quite clearly, innocently, and honestly articulated by Comrade Jeanne Morgan. The first goes as follows:

1. In the competitive sex market which features capitalism, women are obliged to compete with other women for economic security, whether it is in the form of jobs or husbands. Therefore, women do not "indulge" in cosmetics. We are under *social compulsion* to use them.

2. The use of cosmetics is good and necessary because they help to make women beautiful. We have the *right* to use them.

Here *free choice* and the right to use cosmetics are coupled with *social compulsion*. To uphold social compulsion in the name of free choice is contradictory.

The second proposition goes as follows:

1. If Bustelo would spend his time fighting for higher pay, better conditions, better diet, etc. there would be more health and therefore more natural beauty for women. This would "lessen the need for cosmetics."

2. Don't give us the Bustelo standard of natural beauty, which is a "moral beauty" unsuited to modern demands. The world demands cosmetic improvement of beauty, and so long as the world demands it, we have the right to meet that demand.

Here again, free choice in the matter of improved or unimproved beauty is coupled with social compulsion. To support social compulsion in the name of free choice is contradictory.

Bustelo, however, is attacked on the basis of his propositions, devoid of contradictions, as follows: Women are naturally beautiful. Under capitalism, to "gild the lily" is simply to pour billions into the coffers of the profiteers. Beauty is not identical with fashion, but with higher, finer, more enduring values.

Now it is my opinion that some of the comrades are incensed not because they really question the validity of Bustelo's propositions, but because they are caught in the trap of their contradictions and wish Bustelo, or somebody, would help them get out of it. But to do this, we must begin not with an article in the paper on cosmetics, but with *class contradictions* and the class struggle.

A class question

The contradictory position of the comrades arises out of the notion that questions concerning women in the realm of sex, beauty, and so on transcend class lines. The discussion, therefore, is taking place in an abstract void, apart from history and the class struggle. This notion arises out of the bourgeois myth that the needs of all women in the realm of sexual beauty are identical for all classes of women because of their common identity as women.

This is completely false. The *class distinctions* between women transcend their *sex identity* as women. This is above all true in modern capitalist society, the epoch of the sharpest polarization of class forces.

The woman question cannot be divorced from the class question. Any confusion on this score can only lead to erroneous conclusions and setbacks. It will divert the class struggle into a sex struggle of all women against all men.

Historically, the sex struggle was part of the bourgeois feminist movement of the last century. It was a reform movement, conducted within the framework of the capitalist system, and not seeking to overthrow it. But it was a progressive struggle in that women revolted against almost total male domination on the economic, social, and domestic fronts. Through the feminist movement, a number of important reforms were won for women. But the bourgeois feminist movement has run its course, achieved its limited aims, and the problems of today can only be resolved in the struggle of class against class.

The woman question can only be resolved through the lineup of working men and women against the ruling men and women. This means that the interests of the workers as a *class* are identical; and not the interests of all women as a *sex*.

Ruling-class women have exactly the same interest in upholding and perpetuating capitalist society as their men have. The bourgeois feminists fought, among other things, for the right of women as well as men to hold property in their own name. They won this right. Today, plutocratic women hold fabulous wealth in their own names. They are completely in alliance with the plutocratic men to perpetuate the capitalist system. They are not in alliance with the working women, whose needs can only be served through the abolition of capitalism. Thus, the emancipation of working women will not be achieved in alliance with women of the enemy class, but just the opposite; in a struggle *against* them as part and parcel of the whole class struggle. The attempt to identify the interests of all classes of women as a sex takes one of its most insidious forms in the field of female beauty. The bourgeois myth has arisen that since all women want to be beautiful, they all have the same interest in cosmetics and fashions which are currently identified with beauty. To buttress this myth, it is claimed that fashion beauty has prevailed throughout all ages of history and for all classes of women. As evidence, they point to the fact that even in primitive society, women painted and decorated their bodies. To explode this myth, let us briefly examine the history of cosmetics and fashions.

In primitive society, where there were no classes, no economic and social competition, and no sexual competition, the bodies of *both* women and men were painted and "decorated," and it was *not* for the sake of beauty. It was a necessity that arose out of certain primeval and primitive conditions of labor, which I shall explain in detail in future articles.[7]

It was necessary at that time for each individual who belonged to the kinship group to be "marked" as such. These "marks" were not merely ornaments, rings, bracelets, short skirts, etc., but actual gashes, incisions, tattoo marks, etc. as well as different kinds of painting. These marks indicated not only the sex of each individual but the changing age and labor status of each individual as he matured from a child to an elder.

These marks identified the kindred members of the same group or labor collective. Since primitive society was socialist, these marks also expressed *social equality*. The bourgeois anthropologists will not reveal all of this to you, but neither can they reveal anything about the underlying economic and social forces that govern either primitive or modern society.

Then came class society. The marks that signified, among other things, *social equality* under primitive socialism, became transformed into their opposite. They became fashions and decorations that signified *social inequality:* the division of society into rich and poor, into rulers and subjugated. Cosmetics and fashions became the marks of social distinction between the classes and the apex of this social distinction is found in the French Court before the French Revolution.

Among these kings, princes, and landed gentry, *both* men and women were dressed in the height of fashion, with their painted faces, powdered hair, lace ruffles, gold ornaments, and the like. Both sexes were "beautiful" according to the standards of the day. But, more decisively, both sexes in the ruling class were demarcated by these cosmetics and fashions from the peasants who sweated for them on the land and who were, by the same standards, not beautiful. Fashion at that period was the mark of *class distinction* of both sexes of the ruling class against both sexes of the working class.

Then, for certain historical reasons we will not go into here, men left the field of fashion primarily to the women. The big bourgeois, who emerged after the French Revolution, established his class standing through the fashions of his wife, and in other ways, in place of himself wearing gold pants and lace ruffles. Among the women, however, fashions were still the mark of *class* distinction and not *sex* identity in the days of "Judy O'Grady and the Colonel's lady."[8]

But as capitalism developed, there arose an enormous expansion of the productive machine and with it the need for a mass market. Since women represent half the population, profiteers in "beauty" eyed this mass and lusted to exploit it for their own purposes. And so the fashion field was expanded out of the narrow confines of the rich and made socially obligatory upon the whole female population.

Now, for the first time, *class distinctions* were covered over and concealed behind *sex identity*, to serve the needs of this sector of big business. And the bourgeois hucksters began grinding out the propaganda: All women want to be beautiful. Therefore all women have the same interest in cosmetics and fashions. Beauty became identical with fashion and all women were sold on their common "needs and wants" for these fashions.

Today, billions are coined out of every department in the fashion field; cosmetics, clothes, hairdos, slenderizing salons, beauty salons, jewelry, fake and real, and so on. Beauty, it was discovered, was a very flexible formula. All you had to do to become rich was to discover a new aid to beauty and convince the whole population of women that they "needed and wanted" this aid.

To maintain, perpetuate, and expand this profitable field of big business, however, it was necessary to disseminate certain other myths through the propaganda machine at the disposal of the profiteers. These are as follows:

1. Women, from time immemorial, have been competing with other women for sexual attention from the men. Since this is virtually a biological law, from which there is no escape, and since it has existed for all time and will continue to exist for all time, women must submit to their fate and forever compete with each other in the capitalist sex market.

2. In modern society the natural beauty of women does not really count. Indeed, it is insinuated, nature has really abandoned most of the women in the realm of beauty. To make up for their natural disfigurements, they must resort to artificial aids, which the kind profiteers have placed at their disposal.

Let us examine these myths.

Sex competition—natural or social?

Through a study of the sciences of biology and anthropology, we discover that sex competition among women does not exist in nature and did not exist in primitive society.

Sex competition among women is *exclusively* the product of class society and did not exist before class society came into existence, which means for almost a million years of human evolution.

Throughout the animal world there is no such thing as sex competition among females for attention from the males. The only sex competition that prevails in the animal world is that which is inflicted by nature upon the male sex, although it is simply nature's way of assuring perpetuation of the species. Moreover, this natural affliction was eradicated with the building and consolidation of the first human social system, primitive socialism.

The total absence of sex competition among females in nature was one of the reasons why women led in the creation of the first social system, and why the first social system was founded in their image; namely, free from competitive relations. The absence of sex competition among primitive women is unchallenged even by the bourgeois anthropologists. Sometimes, in bewilderment and amazement, it is true, even the reactionary anthropologists point out this "strange peculiarity" or "quaint custom."

But class society succeeded primitive society. Together with the competitive struggle for property and wealth, there arose the competitive struggle among women. But this *social* affliction imposed upon women has nothing natural about it. It is unnatural, and exclusively artificial or social.

Sex competition among women arose with the sex market. The sex market, in turn, arose side by side with the commodity market as a whole. And the commodity market arose with class society. As the commodity market expanded, the standard of female beauty gradually became transformed from natural to artificial, or fashion, beauty. And sex competition developed side by side with this artificial form of beauty, reaching its peak in modern society.

In the earliest period of barter exchange, women were

bartered for cattle and cattle for women. The natural beauty and health of a woman was then at a premium, in the same way and for the same reasons that the natural beauty and health of cattle were at a premium. Both were necessary in the productive and reproductive life of the farm community and the healthiest and most beautiful specimens were best able to carry out their functions.

With the consolidation of the patriarchy and then class society, certain women were accumulated by rich men as one form of all the different kinds of property they were accumulating. These were the concubines. The customs arose of embellishing their natural beauty with decorations and ornaments in the same way and for the same reasons that the palaces were decorated and ornamented. This reached its apex in the Asiatic palaces and harems. These women became the sexual property of the prince or khan, and the more he possessed of those luxury products, the more he gave evidence of his standing as a wealthy man. Sex competition among women moved side by side with and indeed, was even overshadowed in the early days, by property accumulation and competition. It was the buyers of the women who competed with each other for possession of the most beautiful women. The women themselves were sexual property and commodities.

As monogamy displaced polygamy, in the early period property considerations overshadowed sex competition. A rich heiress, regardless of her beauty or health, made a desirable wife to a man accumulating property and vice versa. Naturally, a man would choose, if he had the choice, the more beautiful and healthy woman, but property considerations came first. These marriages, involving property mergers, were conducted in businesslike fashion between the families of the man and woman involved and had only incidental reference to the wishes and desires of the individuals involved. This type of marriage, conducted through family negotiations or a marriage broker, remained in force generally throughout the long agricultural period, when property was primarily landed property.

Then came capitalism, money property, and "free enterprise." This brought free enterprise not only in competitive "free labor" and in business competition but also in female sex competition. In the wealthy class, it is true, marriage mergers continued side by side with property mergers and the two were frequently indistinguishable. Indeed, with the rise of monopoly capitalism, these two kinds of mergers narrowed down the ruling plutocrats to America's "sixty families."

But in America, for certain historical reasons, certain peculiarities arose. Class lines could be transgressed by a man of money, unlike in Europe where class distinctions were established at birth. Thus, a worker or petty bourgeois in the heyday of capitalism here, could by fluke or accident become a rich man and thereby change his class status.

Similarly with a woman. Through fluke or accident, or even the natural endowment of beauty, a woman might marry a millionaire and change her class status. This Cinderella fairy tale, American capitalist style, is most graphically illustrated by Bobo Rockefeller, the miner's daughter.[9]

These peculiarities of American life prepared the psychological ground for the mass commodity market, the mass sex market, and mass sex competition. Just as the Horatio Alger stories became the handbook for men on how to leave your class of rags and enter the class of riches, so with the romance stories for women on how to get and marry the boss's son. Or even the boss himself. All you had to do was rush to the beauty market and buy all the commodities guaranteed to transform you from a Cinderella into a princess.

The fashion world became a capitalist gold mine with virtually unlimited possibilities. All a big businessman had to do was to change the fashions often enough and invent

Advertisement from the 1950s for "up-side-down" refrigerator.

enough new aids to beauty and he could become richer and richer. That is how, under capitalism, the sale of women *as* commodities was displaced by the sale of commodities *to* women. Correspondingly, natural beauty became more and more displaced by artificial beauty; namely, fashion beauty. And that is how the myth arose that beauty is identical with fashion and that all women have identical fashion needs because they all have identical beauty needs.

The fashion profiteers

There are three main gangs of profiteers who batten off the mass of women they dragoon or wheedle into their sex-commodity market in search of beauty:

1. Those who profit by the manipulation of female flesh into the current standardized fashion mold;

2. Those who paint and emulsify this manipulated flesh with cosmetics, dyes, lotions, emulsions, perfumes, etc.;

3. Those who decorate the manipulated and painted flesh with fashionable clothes, jewelry, etc.

In the first category, a woman to be beautiful must be so tall and no taller or shorter. She must weigh so much and not an ounce more or less. She must have certain arbitrary hip, bust, and waist measurements and no other, and so on. If a woman varies from these arbitrary standards, she is not beautiful.

This causes enormous suffering among women who vary from this standardized, assembly-line mold. Weighed down and frustrated by the real burdens of life under capitalism, which they do not understand, they tend to view their beauty "disfigurements" as the source of all their troubles. They become victims of inferiority complexes.

And so they flock by the thousands and tens of thousands to the manipulators of flesh, who put them through various ordeals in their beauty and slenderizing salons. Accompanying them are the face-lifters, nose-bobbers, and other surgical rescuers of female beauty. And new improvements are being added all the time. I am told, for example, that the padded bra has now been improved in that the sponge rubber is inserted directly into the breast through surgical operation. In this way it becomes invisible under "the skin you love to touch."

Through Hollywood stars and beauty contests of all kinds, these fleshly standards are maintained and ballyhooed. As "beauties" they are paraded before the eyes of the hypnotized mass of women through every available means; in the movies, on television, in the slick and pulp magazines. But the monotonous uniformity of these "beauties" is appalling. Every vestige of *variety*, the keynote of real beauty, has been erased. They might as well be so many sugar cookies stamped out of the same dough with the same mold.

Next come the cosmetics dealers, perfumers, dyers, and emulsifiers of this manipulated flesh. Perhaps only the workers in the factories of these cosmetics manufacturers know that the same cheap raw materials that go into the ten-dollar jar or bottle of this and that which is sold in the fancy stores, also go into the fifty-cent bottle or jar. To the naive and innocent, however, the ten-dollar jar must contain some special magic that is not present in the fifty-cent jar. The propaganda machine says so, and so it must be true. These poor women strain their financial resources to get the magic jar, hoping this will transform them from miners' daughters into Rockefeller heiresses.

Finally come the profiteers who decorate and clothe this manipulated and painted flesh. An agonizing choice is placed before the women. Shall they buy for quality or for quantity? The rich, who can do both, have ordained a round-the-clock fashion circus; fashions for mornings, afternoons, cocktails, evening, night, and bedtime. They have ordained a different fashion for "every occasion," but there are endless "occasions." And each hour of the clock and each occasion requires, in addition, a vast collateral assemblage of "accessories," to "go with" whatever they are supposed to go with.

And all this mountain of commodities sold one week, can the next week be declared obsolete through a new fashion decree. Here we get a good example of whether the women get what they need and want, or whether they are compelled to need and want what they get. The *New York Times* recently pointed out that Christian Dior, the famous couturier of the rich, whose styles are copied for the poor, had the power to raise the skirts of *fifty million* American women overnight, or lower them, or both.

This difference of three of four inches in a hemline can convulse the female world, socially obliged to abide by the latest fashions. It may be fun for the rich to throw out their wardrobes and get new ones. But it is disastrous for the poor. Yet it is precisely through such fashion decrees that the profiteers grow fat.

Thus, when the comrades defend the *right* of women to use cosmetics, fashions, etc., without clearly distinguishing between such a right and the capitalist *social compulsion* to use them, they have fallen into the trap of bourgeois propaganda. Even worse, as the vanguard of women, they are leading the mass of women into this fashion rat race and into upholding and perpetuating these profiteers, exploiters, and scoundrels.

Opposition—not adaptation

It is contended that so long as capitalism prevails, we must abide by these cosmetic and fashion decrees. Otherwise, we will be left behind in the economic and social rear. This is true. We must give at least a token recognition of the harsh reality.

But this does not mean that we must accept these edicts and compulsions complacently, or without protest. The workers in the plants are often obliged to accept speedups, pay cuts, and attacks on their unions. But they always and invariably accept them under protest, under continuing struggle against them, and in a constant movement to *oppose* their needs and will against their exploiters.

The class struggle is a movement of *opposition*, not *adaptation*, and this holds true not only of the workers in the plants, but of the women as well, both workers and housewives. It is because the issues are more obscured in the realm of the women as a sex that some of our own comrades have fallen into the trap of adaptation. In this respect we must change our course. Let us begin to demonstrate, through history, that the modern fashion standard of beauty is not a permanent fixture, and that the working woman can and should have something to say about it.

We can point out, for example, that the use of cosmetics by women today is a fairly recent innovation. In the past century, for a woman in search of a husband to use cosmetics was a sure road toward destroying her chances of getting him. In that period, cosmetics was the badge of the prostitute, and no "respectable" man would marry such a woman.

We can point out that some great reforms in women's clothes were achieved as a result of large numbers of women entering the field of social labor after World War I. They cast off their whalebone corsets, the sixteen petticoats, the big pompadours, and the bigger hats, and adopted clothes suited to their working needs. The attractive and useful "casual" clothes of today grew up out of the needs of the working women and were taken over by the rich women for their sports and play. Recently, even the proletarian denim cloth of the factory worker has become socially elevated. Perhaps the rich women were nettled by the sexually attractive appearance of the factory workers in their denim dungarees, overalls, and sweaters, but denim is now made into garments for the rich to wear on their fancy estates.

In this attack on fashions, I am not speaking against good

clothes or even a variety of clothes or even changing the kind of clothes we want to wear. New times, new productive and social conditions will bring changes of all kinds. What I am against is the capitalist rat race of commodity buying that is imposed upon us. As Comrade Jeanne points out, this consumes an inordinate amount of time and attention. Time is the most precious of all raw materials, for time is life. We have better things to do with our lives than dissipate them in this costly, vulgar, and depressing frenzy of fashions.

Under socialism, the question of whether or not a woman wishes to paint and decorate her body will be of no more social consequence than when children today wish to paint up on Halloween and other festive occasions, or when actors paint up for the stage, or when clowns paint up for the circus. Some people may consider them more beautiful when they are painted. Some may not. But this will be a purely personal opinion and nothing more. There will be no more *social compulsion* for all women to become painted and decorated regiments. Therefore, let us not defend this fashion regimentation in the name of "beauty."

Beauty, art, and labor

Fashions are not immortalized by the artists as beauty. On the contrary, the artists are concerned with totally different values and standards. There is common agreement on the enduring values in art and these enduring values are established when art corresponds most closely to life itself in its changing historical phases, in its changing moods.

The artists hold up the mirror to life in a reflective mood or in anger or compassion or sardonic humor. They seek to capture the joy and sorrow of life; its strength and weakness, its evils and grandeurs. When these moods and values are captured by the artists, their productions become works of art and of beauty. Great art, among other things, reflects the class struggle. And great art is beauty.

Among the forms of beauty captured by the artists, is the beauty of the human form. But this includes *both* sexes and *all ages*. The Greeks, in their statues, portrayed the beauty of the male as well as the female form. Neither sex was represented in cosmetics and fashions. On the walls of the art galleries, human beauty is found in pictures of old women and old men, of the very young, of the sweated peasants and proletariat. Beauty is an expression of the *variety* as well as poignancy of life and of people. It is not an expression of fashion juvenility and vapidity.

There is one form of "beauty" which has not been and never will be captured by the artists. And that is the dummy in the fancy shop windows which we see in its ridiculous human form on the fashionable streets and in the fashionable houses. The artists do not consider this dummy beautiful and they are quite right. Portraits are painted of these human dummies, but they are painted for the sake of money not for the sake of beauty.

Thus, when Bustelo pointed out the heroic pioneer woman of America as an example of beauty, he was singling out a good example. It is, indeed, a "moral beauty" and a truthful beauty. And it is also true that this beauty represents *our* morals and *our* truth, for it does not represent the morals and truth of the hucksters. But in the realm of genuine beauty, is there any other kind than that which rests upon *our* morals and *our* truth?

I applaud Bustelo as a man who hasn't been sold on the huckster standards of beauty and whose sense of the real beauty of women remains fresh and clean. Such men are to be admired and not sneered at. We want more such men to help us emancipate women from the bourgeois mire of tinsel and trash. Together with such men we can hold up *our* standard of beauty.

Beauty has no identity with fashions. But it has an identity with *labor*. Apart from the realm of nature, all that is beautiful has been produced in labor and by the laborers. Outside the realm of nature, beauty does not exist apart from labor and never will. For the beauty of all the products of labor, and of all the arts produced in and through labor, are incorporated within these products and these arts.

Humanity itself, together with the beauty of humanity, was produced in and through the labor process. As Engels pointed out, when the humans *produced,* they produced themselves as *humans.* They cast off their apelike appearance and became more and more beautiful. When the capitalist social disfigurement of exploited labor is removed, the true beauty of labor and of the laborers will stand forth in their true dimensions.

It is only in class society that the myth has grown up that *labor* is identical with *exploited labor.* This myth serves the needs of the ruling class which maintains itself as a parasitic excrescence on the backs of the workers. Through the identity they make between labor and exploited labor, they perpetuate a split between *producers* and *consumers,* glorifying the latter at the expense of the former. The less you produce and the more you consume, the higher you rise in the world of the snobs and the idle rich. Not labor but the conspicuous waste of the products of labor is the mark of capitalist social distinction.

But this did not always exist, despite their propaganda to the contrary. In primitive society, where exploited labor was unknown, there was no split between producers and consumers. Every member of society produced, according to his age and ability, and every member of society shared in consuming their productions and in the enjoyment of them in common. Social value and distinction were registered in the realm of production, and that is why the women of primitive society were so valuable and regarded so highly. They labored and taught the arts of labor and carried on the traditions of labor and advanced labor to ever higher levels of production.

To cover up their empty, vapid, parasitic existence, the idle rich of capitalist society propagate the notion that the idle life is the "good life" and the "beautiful life." As evidence, they hold up their flabby, lily-white hands with long red fingernails as tokens of "beauty," and the "good life."

What a mockery this is of the gift of labor—the primary creative force of humanity. The truth is, the idle life is the most corrosive and corrupting of all influences upon the mental, moral, physical, and psychological fiber of human beings. Without labor, whether of hand or brain—and these are interdependent—humans rot away. Without labor, the human is less than the potato in the ground and does not deserve the gift of humanity.

One of our tasks is to overthrow this bourgeois lie that labor is identical with exploited labor. Another is to restore labor to its rightful place as the most honorable, the most necessary, the most useful and beautiful of all human attributes. In the process we will destroy the split between art and labor. In primitive society there was no such split. These were two forms of labor and both forms created beauty. In the coming socialist society, we will make a return to this harmony between art, labor, and beauty.

Under socialism, when the workers take command of society, they will decide what labor is valid and what is not. They will make everything that is necessary, useful, and beautiful to serve their needs. But beyond that they will not be the slaves of *things* as the property accumulators of capitalist society are. They will be occupied with higher aims, loftier goals, and far more interesting occupations and preoccupations than the scramble after fashions in houses and clothing. There will be a new outpouring of productive, scientific, and artistic achievement for *social* advancement and not personal greed. For these socialist workers will be the conquerors not only of this planet, but of the universe.

Those who wallow in bourgeois propaganda cannot see this kind of future. It is our task to show it to them.

The massive propaganda machine

As the capitalist commodity market expanded, more and more attention was directed toward the population of women as important buyers of consumer goods of all kinds; homes and home furnishings, wearing apparel for themselves and their children; maternity needs before, during, and after the birth of babies; their sexual beauty needs in holding the love and attention of husbands, and so on.

Many of the useful products sold as commodities are genuine necessities for these women and their families. As such, they do not need to be "sold" through expensive advertising and promotional campaigns. But under the anarchistic system of "free enterprise," with its enormous unnecessary duplication of products, the various manufacturers and dealers compete with each other to gain access to this women's market. This has produced the huckster field, a parasitic adjunct to big business and in itself another form of big business. The hucksters not only tout the different wares for sale, but they are also part of the propaganda machine that disseminates bourgeois and petty-bourgeois ideology.

The propaganda machine as a whole is a vast institution. It has control of the mass arenas for selling commodities and bourgeois ideology: the radio, television, but above all the press. Capitalist newspapers and magazines are built around and maintained by the pages of advertising. In addition to the general press and publications a large number of magazines, directed exclusively to women, came into existence over the past years and have been advancing with giant strides. These are the "slick" magazines.

Production-wise these magazines are very handsome indeed. Beautiful color plates of luscious commodities of all kinds are reproduced on the finest of slick papers. But the contents are also slick. They sell not only all the profitable merchandise guaranteed to enrich big business, but they also sell capitalist propaganda in the slickest and most subtle manner.

Some of these slick magazines are frankly directed to the top class of bourgeois women and make no bones about it. Others, however, are aimed at a larger field. The most successful of these national magazines are those which are best able to identify the needs of all women on the basis of their identity as a sex.

Much of the editorial space in these magazines is given over to the maternity needs of married women and to problems connected with home and family. But as more and more women entered the field of social labor, white-collar workers, career women, and even industrial workers came in for increasing attention.

"Scientists" and "specialists" of all kinds were produced to write articles for all the different kinds of women. These professors and writers deliver homilies on child care, mother care, family relations, husband and wife relations, etc. Other specialists discuss problems connected with career women. The career woman is pitted against the housewife and vice versa, leaving both with a sense of frustration and dissatisfaction. For all women, there are prominent doctors, psychiatrists, and others to discuss problems concerning sex, psychiatry, and other matters of this kind.

All of these articles, some of them containing interesting facts and figures and some of them even bordering on good sense, are completely abstract; namely, totally devoid of any concrete reference to class relations and the class struggle. Writers who wish to discuss these class questions are not invited into the pages of these slick magazines. Thus, the "science" that is peddled in these magazines is exclusively bourgeois science, analyzed with the bourgeois method and aiming at bourgeois goals.

In both the advertising and editorial sections of these magazines there are beautiful color plates depicting the "great American dream come true." There are pictures of the beautiful, streamlined American family, composed of a glamorous father and mother and two streamlined children standing near their streamlined car, television set, refrigerator, or some other product. Or we find the streamlined career woman enjoying the sea breezes on a streamlined ship or at a glamorous vacation resort and so on.

The poor housewives and low-paid white-collar workers, who view all this in the pages of these beautiful magazines, are torn by unrest and discontent of all kinds. What is the matter with them as *women*, which dispossesses them from this "great American dream"? Why is it a phantom for them instead of a reality? Not understanding their problems as *class* problems, they view them as *sex* problems and develop more inferiority complexes.

Large sections of housewives and white-collar workers do not identify their interests with the proletariat. On the other hand they cannot identify themselves except in imagination with the rich bourgeois women. They chafe and churn, having none of the advantages of the proletariat such as their unification into trade unions and yet none of the advantages of the bourgeoisie. The middle class is indeed a class torn by contradictions, situated as it is between the two class poles.

Our task is to win this lower middle class of housewives and low-paid white-collar workers. We must break the hypnosis of the bourgeois ideology under which they suffer. We must teach these women that their interests lie with the working class. And we must show them the road to the working class.

But this task cannot be carried out if we ourselves fall bait to big business propaganda and ideology. To accept the capitalist standards in any field is to uphold capitalist ideology.

To accept its ideology is to accept the capitalist system as a whole. Any attempt of any kind to find a common ground or identity between us and the class enemy can only lead to a petty-bourgeois infection.

That this infection may already exist is revealed in Comrade McGowan's contribution to the Bustelo discussion. Here is her description of the "American beauty":

> The long-stemmed American beauty, full of natural vitality and physical grace, with shining hair, clear eyes, smooth skin, and natural cosmetics with a trace of accent here and there, is no fiction but an American commonplace. This type of beauty is the American social standard, whatever Bustelo might think of it, but by and large it is the exclusive property of first of all youth, and secondly of wealth.

There is no doubt that this is the capitalist social standard. But I know what I think of it. I think it sounds like a description of the female counterpart of the Nordic hero, of the female white supremacist. Where, in this "standard" of beauty is there any place for the dark-skinned Negro woman with kinky hair, or the short-stemmed woman of the Puerto Rican, Jewish, Japanese, and other European and Asiatic races, all of whom make up the working population of this country? In my opinion they are all more beautiful than the model set before us by Comrade McGowan.

It is a short step from becoming lyrical over this American beauty to becoming lyrical over the capitalist system which has produced it. How short this step is, is spelled out by Comrade McGowan:

> The revolution in technology and science, which reached its highest development under capitalism in the last forty years or so, has wrought a partial revolution in

all phases of life—in the relation between the sexes, in sexual morality, in medicine, in nutrition and health, in architecture, in art, in beauty, in hobbies for leisure, in city planning, in child rearing, in methods of education, in psychology—a revolution in life and in living. . . .

In this epoch of the mounting evils of capitalism, of its death agony, with all the crucial issues of war, depression, fascism still unresolved, Comrade McGowan tells us we have been living through a period of *capitalist revolution,* with everything virtually solved except for a few minor touches here and there. This proposition is taken lock, stock, and barrel out of the slick magazines, just as her standard of beauty comes from that source.

Jack Bustelo

The fetish of cosmetics

Is the use of cosmetics worth the attention of a Marxist? At first sight, it might seem we should say no. What difference does a question seemingly so remote from the class struggle, really make? After all, the great problems of unemployment, fascism, war, and the struggle for power reduce everything else to subordinate importance. And surely, in the list of subordinate questions that Marxists do feel constrained to consider, cosmetics comes at least close to the bottom. Yet among readers of the *Militant* recently, a minor article, aimed at no more than showing how the "recession" had affected the cosmetics business and what the hucksters intended to do about it, evoked the kind of response that only an important issue deserves. How are we to explain this?

A possible answer is that I displayed prejudice against women in writing about the cosmetics purveyors and their "public relations" department and that this display of prejudice in the *Militant* naturally aroused indignation. (An example: "Maybe you, Jack, want to laugh and ridicule my using popular cosmetics to overcome some of these difficulties of working for a living. Laugh if you want. . . ."—F.J. in the *Militant*.) I must admit that the accusation is not easy for me to answer. First, the evidence that I was guilty of prejudice is not submitted. How then can I decide rationally who is at fault, myself or the critics, or whether an element of misunderstanding is involved? Moreover, in the absence of explanation as to what my prejudice consisted of, I am given no opportunity for self-correction.

The absence of a specific indication as to the prejudice leads me to suspect that only feeling is involved in the side of my critics, a feeling that perhaps does not correspond with the real facts. In this predicament I may be excused perhaps for referring to what Hegel had to say about judgments that are not made explicit: "Since the man of common sense appeals to his feeling, to an oracle within his breast, he is done with anyone who does not agree. He has just to explain that he has no more to say to anyone who does not find and feel the same as himself. In other words, he tramples the roots of humanity underfoot. For the nature of humanity is to impel men to agree with one another, and its very existence lies simply in the explicit realization of a community of conscious life. What is antihuman, the condition of mere animals, consists in keeping within the sphere of feeling pure and simple, and in being able to communicate only by way of feeling-states."

Whether we agree or disagree that I am consciously or unconsciously prejudiced for or against women, the key issues of the dispute over cosmetics still remain and have to be considered on their own merits. A discussion of these issues I think will prove fruitful no matter what nuances of differences over them we may finally end up with.

'Cosmetics are a grim necessity'

In her letter to the *Militant*, Helen Baker of Seattle says: "Far from being a luxury (and they are taxed as such), cosmetics are a grim necessity for the older or not physically blessed woman worker." Leaving aside the relation between cosmetics and the older or not physically blessed woman worker, which I will consider later, I agree completely with Comrade Baker's conclusion that "cosmetics are a grim necessity." They are a grim necessity in the current decades of capitalism, particularly in the United States. Just how grim it is we will see presently, but let us start with the necessity.

This was well expressed by Antoinette Konikow, one of the pioneer American Trotskyists,[10] in a letter in the June 9, 1945, *Militant* called to my attention by Gustie Dante of Boston. The letter, which seems aimed at partially correcting an article by Grace Carlson in the April 21, 1945, *Militant* is worth quoting in full:

> Your article on "The Right to Be Beautiful," in which you discuss the use of cosmetics and beauty aids, awoke a few thoughts that I should like to share with your readers. I have lived for almost three-quarters of a century and in my youth we never used cosmetics. In fact, the use of them was considered indecent. And still we had beauty and romance. How do you explain the present situation? It seems to me that woman's entry into industry has a great deal to do with it.
>
> While rich ladies use cosmetics to cover up their pale faces acquired during Society's winter whirl of endless nights of drinking and dancing, women who work in factories and shops have pale and tired faces because of physical exhaustion due to overwork, bad air, hurried lunches, and their whole life of rush and worry.
>
> The working woman uses cosmetics, not only for her own satisfaction—to have a nice appearance or to attract possible romance—but she has to look well and attractive to keep her job. I think that if women would lead a healthy and normal life, their faces would look different.

They would acquire the rosy cheeks that we had in our youth and the bright eyes and the red lips.

To me cosmetics are an expression of our unhealthy life under capitalism. It is not an important issue but it is just as well to understand that changes in women's work affect even the most minute forms of their life. This doesn't mean that I condemn cosmetics. I think that we shall have to use them for quite a while yet!

Despite its shortness, this letter says a great deal. Note especially the last paragraph: "To me cosmetics are an expression of our unhealthy life under capitalism." It is quite clear that just as Antoinette could recall that in her youth beauty existed without cosmetics so she could visualize a time in the future when beauty would again exist without cosmetics. Her attitude was revolutionary. At the same time, so far as a woman has to use cosmetics "to keep her job" or for "her own satisfaction," Antoinette didn't condemn cosmetics. This necessity, she recognized, is forced on us by the times and we have to bow to it "for quite a while yet."

But do cosmetics bestow beauty?

The necessity of using cosmetics will be granted, I think, by almost everyone. We also have to use money. But then a most important question arises. Do our norms of beauty include either money or cosmetics?

Comrade Jeanne Morgan of Los Angeles starts, I think, from the same grounds as I do when she says, "Our use of cosmetics is far from an indulgence—it is basically an economic necessity. . . ." However, she then draws the following conclusion: "and from this has become an aesthetic necessity."

All right, but an aesthetic necessity to what class in what kind of society? If we were to continue the train of thought indicated by Antoinette Konikow we would have to say that it is an aesthetic necessity in capitalist society, one that is *imposed* on us insofar as we can't escape that society. Knowing this, however, we no longer consider it beautiful. We have a different norm as class-conscious workers just as our norm of morality is different from that of the capitalists.

But Comrade Morgan puts cosmetics in a suprahistorical category: "Cosmetics are ancient, and have been used for many reasons, good and bad. They will probably be used even under socialism, by both men and women, for the pleasure of personal adornment."

Let's put it in a somewhat different way: It's human nature to use cosmetics for the pleasure of adornment. People have always wanted this pleasure and always will. You can't change human nature.

If we were to agree to this, what happens to the grounds we started out with in common, that our "use of cosmetics is far from an indulgence—it is basically an economic necessity . . ."? Isn't it obvious that to take the view that cosmetics bestow beauty is to make a concession to bourgeois ideology?

The language of cosmetics

Up to now we have talked *about* cosmetics without permitting them to speak for themselves; yet there are few sectors of the commodity world gifted with more eloquent tongues. Let us pause in our discussion long enough to hear a word from them; and taking a hint from Comrade Morgan let us turn the floor over to a cosmetic used—not by the socialist man of the future—but by the capitalist and proletarian men of the present.

When my electric razor breaks down, I go back to the old safety razor. Afterward I splash on a cosmetic that stings at first but seems to help take away the raw feeling you get from scraping a razor across your hide. I bought it because it says "fifty percent alcohol" on the label and legend has it that alcohol reduces the chances of infection from using a razor. On the back of the label is a short message in which Mennen Skin Bracer tells about itself. It is demagogically silent about the risk and annoyance of shaving. It doesn't say a single word about the *economic necessity* that compels me to go through the daily ritual in order to keep a job. Instead, it proclaims:

"A delightful after-shave lotion. Cooling, refreshing, mildly astringent. A pleasant easy-to-use deodorant. Use Skin Bracer any time of the day or night—it peps you up. And the intriguing aroma wows the ladies!"

That last sentence is intriguing isn't it? If it were really true, think how simplified some of life's problems could become for our hardworking proletarian. When he comes home unstrung from the terrific pace of eight hours on the belt line and goes to the bathroom to pep himself up with Mennen Skin Bracer, he suddenly sees the way out. No more drab, endless perspectives of a lifetime of poverty and toil. He shaves with a new sparkle in his eyes, puts on the intriguing aroma, goes to the right part of town, astutely sidles around an heiress until he gets her downwind, "wows" her, and from then on lives the life of Riley. Why even Bustelo might use a dash of the intriguing stuff and wow the women who think he is prejudiced against their sex. Isn't it sheer sorcery what magic has been captured and sealed in a bottle of Mennen Skin Bracer?

Now surely the public relations department of the Mennen Company wouldn't put something on millions of bottles that no man would possibly believe. But what is it that the men users of the cosmetic are induced to believe? Obviously that there is a *thing* that can help smooth out their relations with women. And that means, doesn't it, that there is something basically wrong on a wide scale in the *relations* between men and women? What is it? And what is its cause?

Lest we jump to a too hasty generalization from insufficient cases, let's try another cosmetic. In September, Max Factor ran an advertisement in the newspapers for a "color-fast" lipstick, "to make men go mad over you," says the ad, "wear See Red." This lipstick "is a rich, true shade—a hot-tempered red that can make *you* maddeningly pretty. Looks fiery bright for hours and hours, too—amazing 'stay-on lustre' won't fade or blot away. Come in for See Red today. But careful—don't start anything you can't finish!" The accompanying illustration shows two men forehead to forehead, pushing their noses against each other like two stars seeing red at the Marigold wrestling matches and a girl, her lips highly colored, looking sidelong at them with a kind of pyromaniacal pleasure.

Again we note the demagogic silence about the economic necessity of wearing lipstick. Nothing is even said about the lipstick making you look young. The emphasis is not at all on how lipstick helps you get and hold a job. The emphasis is on how "to make men go mad over you."

Again we ask what sorcery it is that has captured and sealed this magic power in a few inches of colored grease. And we have to say that the sorcery is in the fact that a *thing* can be endowed with the capacity to smooth out women's relations with men. We are forced to add to our conclusions that from the side of women something must be basically wrong on a wide scale with their *relations* with the opposite sex.

Let us try one more, a recent half-page ad. Two drawings: A reclining nude woman discreetly seen from the rear—a bottle of perfume called "ishah." Sandwiched above and below these eye-pullers are the following sensational words: "The very essence of woman—Her beauty—Her allure—*ishah*—discovered by Charles of the Ritz. Bottled, packaged, sealed in France—$10 to $12.50 (plus tax)."

This is not a new scientific discovery enabling a lonely man to buy the very essence of woman, her beauty, her allure, all bottled, packaged, and sealed in France. It is aimed at women. Are you a woman who is not a woman? Has no beauty? No allure? Take heart. All this has been fixed up now. The very essence of woman, her beauty, her allure has now been discovered, captured, and sealed in a bottle. Everything that all the different kinds of cosmetics and beauty-aid gadgets offer is now available in a single bottle from $10 to $12.50 (plus tax). And it's all marvelously easy, no inconvenience, no plastic surgery, no torture. Just touch a drop or two of the essence behind your ears and WOW!

Long ago in analyzing the strange powers of money, Marx called attention to this projection by which human beings see their relations not as relations but as *things* which they endow with remarkable powers. Indicating the parallel to certain magic objects in primitive beliefs and religions he called it *fetishism*. What we have in cosmetics is a fetish, a particular fetish in the general fetishism that exists in the world of commodities. The special power that cosmetics have derives from the fact that in addition to economic relations, sexual relations attach to them. That is the real source of the "beauty" both men and women see in cosmetics.

The duality of cosmetics

As we can see by now, the use of cosmetics, although it need not be placed among the unsmiling questions, has a most serious side from the viewpoint of Marxist philosophy. Every student of *Capital* who has really pondered over the "The Fetishism of Commodities and the Secret Thereof" will know what I mean.[11] But even without going into it that deeply I think it is possible to grasp the essence of the matter through a special case with which most people are familiar.

At a certain age, girls—sometime very young ones—begin trying out lipstick, powder, and rouge. In almost every case, this either causes or is associated with a sharpening of relations with their parents. At the same time they often seem to leap ahead of their age group so far as their former boy associates are concerned. If they can get away with it, they go out with youths considerably older than they are. The reason such girls use cosmetics is to facilitate this *by appearing older than they are.*

What they seek to say is quite obvious. Through the magic of cosmetics they express their wish to cut short their childhood and youth and achieve the most desirable thing in the world—adulthood. Why they want to be adults can be surmised in the light of how capitalist society treats its youth. Precisely at the age when the sexual drives begin to appear and an intense need is felt for both knowledge and experience, capitalist society denies both of them. Just when the developing human being must set out to establish normal relations with the opposite sex, capitalist society through the family intervenes and attempts to suppress the urge.

The relation with the other sex thus tends to become distorted and the interest that belongs to the relation shifts to a considerable degree to a symbol. The powers and allure of the relation—some at least—are likewise transferred to the symbol. Lipstick, for instance, comes to signify adulthood; that is, the adult capacity and freedom to engage in activities forbidden to children. By smearing her lips the child says, this gives me the power to do what I want. Naturally it's only a wish and an imaginary satisfaction—or at least that's what most parents imagine it to be or wish to rate it as, and the real power of the drive toward relations with the opposite sex, disguised by the fetish, is not always recognized. The symbol becomes beautiful or ugly, beneficent or malignant. In Antoinette Konikow's youth, for instance, lipstick was "indecent." Today it is a "must."

This interesting alternation in time of the aesthetics of cosmetics is accompanied by an even more striking duality in its powers. To a child, as we have noted, cosmetics are a means of hiding and disguising youth, a means of appearing

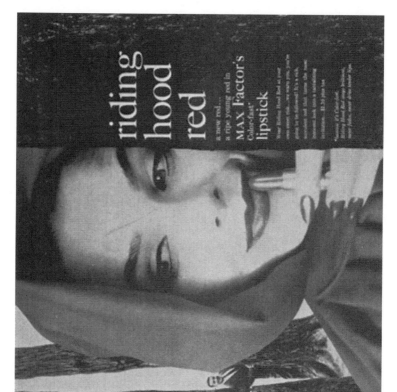

riding
hood
red

a new red...
a ripe young red in
MAX Factor's
Color-fast
lipstick

...to bring the wolves out...

This and facing page are typical cosmetics advertisements of the 1950s; very little has changed since then in advertising.

to be at the age when it is socially acceptable to gratify the urge for knowledge and especially experience in sexual relations. Thus the same fetish displays opposite powers at one and the same time—the power to make old women young and young women old. Mother uses cosmetics to hide her age and bring out her youth by covering up the dark circles under her eyes. Daughter uses them to hide her youth and even touches up her eyes with blue shading to bring out her adult beauty.

Now what shall we say of children who use cosmetics because of the social necessity to look old: Shall they be denied that right? My inclination would be to go ahead and use cosmetics if they feel like it. At the same time I would be strongly tempted to explain what a fetish is, how it comes to be constructed, what is really behind it and how this particular society we live in denies youth the most elementary right of all—the right to grow naturally into a normal sexual relationship—and gives them instead the fetish of cosmetics as an appropriate companion to the fetish of money.

The application of Marxist method has thus forced cosmetics to yield two important results. We find ourselves touching two problems of utmost moment in capitalist society—the interrelation of men and women and the interrelation of youth and adults; that is, the whole problem of the family. In addition, we have discovered that these interrelations as shaped by capitalist society are bad, for it is from the lack of harmony and freedom in them that the fetish of cosmetics arises. Existence of the fetish, in turn, helps maintain the current form of interrelations by creating a diversionary channel and an illusory palliative. Thus we have uncovered a vicious cycle. Bad interrelations feeds the fetish of cosmetics; the fetish of cosmetics feeds bad interrelations.

Our application of Marxist method has given us even more. If we deny that beauty is inherent in a *thing*, then it must be found in a human relation; or at least its source must be found in such a relation. Doesn't that mean that the beauty associated with sex is at bottom the beauty not of a thing but of a relation? If we want to understand that beauty we must seek it first in the truth of the relation; that is, through science. Is it really so difficult to see that in the society of the future, the society of socialism where all fetishes are correctly viewed as barbaric, that beauty will be sought in human relationships and that after science has turned its light into the depths that seem so dark to us—the depths of the mind—the great new arts will be developed in those virgin fields?

Intimations of it in the class society that is our heritage may be seen, I believe, in such relationships as Marx and Engels achieved. Whether they were fully aware of it we do not know. But we ourselves touch such forms of beauty, I think, in a one-sided way in the admiration and love we feel for our comrades in the socialist struggle. It is their *character* that attracts us, not the smoothness of their complexion, the regularity of their features, their age, or the color of their skin. And character, as we all know, is determined in action, that is by the deeds we perform. That is where a revolutionary socialist looks for beauty in people.

'The corporate taste'

Antoinette Konikow, let us recall, noted that in her youth girls never used cosmetics. "And still we had beauty and romance." This may sound strange to us in this day and age, particularly if we have come to regard cosmetics as a sign of beauty and romance. What has caused us to adopt this attitude?

We might find hints as to the reason from the theoretical point of view if we carefully searched the Marxist classics. George Plekhanov, in his *Fundamental Problems of Marxism*, for instance, notes the following about a previous period:

E. Chesneau's book *Les chefs d'école*, Paris, 1883, 378–79, contains the following subtle observation regarding the romanticists' psychology. The author points out that romanticism made its appearance after the Revolution and the Empire. "In literature and in art there was a crisis similar to that which occurred in morals after the Terror—a veritable orgy of the senses. People had been living in fear, and that fear had gone. They gave themselves up to the pleasures of life. Their attention was taken up exclusively with external appearances and forms. Blue skies, brilliant lights, the beauty of women, sumptuous velvet, iridescent silk, the sheen of gold, and the sparkle of diamonds filled them with delight. People lived only with the eyes . . . they had stopped thinking." This has much in common with the psychology of the times we are living through in Russia. In both cases, however, the course of events leading up to this state of mind was itself the outcome of the course of economic development.[12]

The period Plekhanov refers to was a period of reaction such as we are living in, the difference being that the reaction we are suffering from is incomparably deeper than the one that afflicted the Russian socialists. Plekhanov's hint might well direct a study on this question, particularly on how the weight of the reaction affects the revolutionary vanguard through such indirect avenues as capitalist norms of beauty. In place of sumptuous velvets, iridescent silks, the sheen of gold, the sparkle of diamonds, we could readily substitute sumptuous ranch houses, iridescent TV screens, the sheen of a new automobile, and the sparkle of tile in a modern kitchen. There would be no lack of material!

We would even enjoy a considerable advantage over Chesneau and Plekhanov, for the influence of capitalist norms appears to be far more direct in America than it was in either Russia or France.

For example, take the following ad from the latest issue of *Charm* magazine (October 1954): A glamorized photograph of a conventional female beauty on a date to see "The Pajama Game" with a conventional male beauty. (Both of them are the long-stemmed Aryan type.) And here is the message: "Alive after five . . . thanks to her Remington Electric typewriter. And no wonder—*electricity does the work*—helps today's smart women of letters turn out such truly beautiful work in *so little time,* with *so little effort* and so pleasing to the boss." This is accompanied by a picture of the fetish itself—a brand new electric Remington typewriter, artfully streamlined to make it wind resistant.

The reference to the relationship behind the fetish ("The Pajama Game") is not what makes this a remarkable ad. It is the inference that a typist, stenographer, or secretary can leave the office more dead than alive. This and the open admission that the really interested party is the boss. A fetish that permits a speedup ("so little time") is ballyhooed almost like an after-shave lotion. Compare the "it peps you up" of Mennen Skin Bracer with the "alive after five" of a Remington Rand typewriter. What sorcery there is in the typewriter of a huckster!

Lest anyone still doubt how directly the American capitalist class is involved in this question of beauty, let me quote the following words from a recently published book, *The Tastemakers,* written by one of them, Russell Lynes, managing editor of *Harper's* magazine:

"There are pressures on our tastes from all sides, pressures that even the most reluctant among us can scarcely ignore. The making of taste in America is, in fact, a major industry. Is there any other place you can think of where there are so many professionals telling so many nonprofessionals what their taste should be? Is there any country which has as many magazines as we have devoted to telling people how they should decorate their homes, clothe their bodies, and deport themselves in company? And so many newspaper columns full of hints about what is good taste and what is bad taste? In the last century and a quarter the purveying of taste in America has become big business, employing hundreds of thousands of people in editorial and advertising offices, in printing plants, in galleries and museums, in shops and consultants' offices. If the taste industry were to go out of business we would have a major depression, and there would be breadlines of tastemakers as far as the eye could see."

That strikes me as pretty plain speaking about the source of one of the pressures bearing down on us. However, Lynes puts it still more baldly in the very next paragraph:

"This is not, however, a catastrophe we are likely to encounter, because the taste industry has gradually become essential to the operation of our American brand of capitalism. It is in the nature of our economic system not merely to meet demand but to create it. One of the ways that demand is created is by changing people's tastes, or at least inviting them to change, and by making the pressures to give up what seemed good yesterday for what should seem inviting today so strong that they are almost impossible to resist."

How difficult the pressures are to resist we may judge from cases of good revolutionists who succumbed to the prosperity that has endured since the outbreak of World War II. Some of them did it silently, without seeking to find a political difference as excuse or rationalization. The lure of a ranch house in the suburbs with a picture window as laid out in the lush colors of *Better Homes and Gardens* proved impossible to resist. The overwhelming pressure has a name; it is "bourgeois." The proletarian became "bourgeoisified." In other words, he gave up thinking and became an addict of the opium of commodity fetishism.

Lynes describes the days we live in as the days of "the corporate taste." "The corporation has, in fact," he says, "become one of the most powerful and conscientious (does he mean "conscious"?) art patrons of our day, and has established itself not only as a purveyor of tasteful objects but as an arbiter of taste as well." He even dates the beginning of "the corporate taste": "It was inevitable that sooner or later business, in its efforts to reestablish itself in the confidence of the public, would embrace culture. And this it began to do in earnest in the early 1940s while the war was on."

The imperialist war thus had its reflection in the development of an imperialist taste in culture in America.

"If we are to understand this influence of the corporation on the taste of our time, there are three ways in which the corporation must be looked at—as a consumer of the arts, in its role as patron; as a purveyor of the arts, in its role as the manufacturer or dispenser of the objects with which we surround ourselves; and finally as a new kind of society in which taste has a new kind of significance." This managing editor of an influential bourgeois magazine obviously knows what it is all about. He even admits that the motive of the corporations in the field of culture "no matter how indirectly expressed, has been profit."

He cites examples of forays in this field by such corporations as Dole Pineapple, Capehart Phonograph-Radio, the Container Corporation of America, Standard Oil of New Jersey, the Pepsi-Cola Company, and Corning Glass. And he explains in some detail what the calculations of these patrons of the beautiful are:

"To a great many manufacturers the problem is not how to improve taste but how to keep it fluid so that what looked new and attractive last year will seem old-fashioned this year and downright archaic ten years from now."

"Just as the public relations counselor is concerned with the corporation's psychological warfare, the industrial designer is concerned with the logistics of taste. His function in other words is to fight the corporation's battles on the taste front."

It is a temptation to continue citing Lynes to show how consciously American big business goes about fixing and unfixing our ideas of beauty, but one more paragraph will have to suffice:

"It is the men who make and sell refrigerators and rugs, automobiles and baby carriages, furniture and dresses whose sales charts would have a dismal downward inclination to the right unless they managed to redesign their wares in ways that make last year's 'latest word' seem today's drab cliché. An 'old-fashioned' stove with its oven at a reasonable eye level may be more efficient than a brand-new one that forces the housewife to bend double to see the roast, but the manufacturer will do his best to make her long for a new model because it is more 'up to date' and, euphemistically, 'better designed.' The same is, of course, true of automobiles—even more true. Ever since 1905 the automobile industry has been second only to the women's fashion industry in its insistence on the glamour of 'this year's model' compared with 'last year's model.' In fact, a man clothes himself in his car in much the same spirit that a woman dresses herself in her clothes, and he is subject to the calculated whims of Detroit just as his wife is subject to the equally calculated whims of Paris."

In the whole history of capitalism, has the bourgeoisie ever gone about cultivating the fetish of commodities more coldbloodedly than American big business?

"Art has pervaded all phases of life," Marjorie McGowan declares, criticizing my exposure of the cosmetics peddlers. "Pots, pans, fabrics, furniture, lamps, stoves, landscaping, architecture—*all* objects in the environment have become mediums for the creative expression of the artist and the designer." I must admit that there is a grain of truth in what she says. It is "corporate art"—perhaps best exemplified in the singing commercial—that has pervaded all phases of life in America today.

Should we accept battle on this front?

Marjorie McGowan accepts the "logistics" of the corporation battle on the taste front as a "revolution in living." I appreciate her frankness and think she does the party a service by stating precisely what her views are on this question, for it is bound to help all of us in clarifying our attitude in this difficult field. But I must add that critical as she is of my exposure of the cosmetics hucksters and profiteers and my subsequent letter in the *Militant,* she is uncritical in a more important direction. "Socialism, for instance," she says, "will not throw out the morality of bourgeois society in toto and create a new one out of the whole cloth. . . . Rather, socialism will extract the hypocrisy and the mysticism out of bourgeois morality and leave the universal ideals of human brotherhood and make a reality of the Golden Rule."

I will not belabor the point of how far this departs from the view of the authors of the *Communist Manifesto* who held that the socialist revolution "involves the most radical rupture with traditional ideas."[13] I am sure that on thinking it over, Comrade McGowan will agree that she has conceded to bourgeois morality more than is its due. The ideals of human brotherhood are the very antithesis of bourgeois morality—not the morality they preach on Sunday, naturally, but the morality they practice 365 days of the year—which puts naked self-interest above all other considerations as we have seen even in the case of cosmetics. The ideals of human brotherhood are incompatible with the norms of any class society.

Marxists have been critical of bourgeois standards of morals and beauty from the beginning. Today in America where the most powerful capitalist class of all time has decided quite consciously to pay some attention to aesthetics it is not simply a theoretical duty to meet them on this field; it is a burning practical necessity. It is part and parcel of the whole ideological offensive we must conduct to maintain our

Marxist heritage and build a combat party. We cannot leave this field to the bourgeoisie!

However, it might be objected that this is a hopeless struggle. "We are not going to change the world by revolting against such a sideline issue as this—and that seems to be what your article would have us do," declares Jeanne Morgan. "If working-class women boycotted all cosmetics I doubt very much if it would help build a labor party or lessen Jim Crow or halt the war drive." (By this time, I hope, it is unnecessary to explain that I don't advocate "boycotting" cosmetics any more than I advocate boycotting money.)

F.J. likewise is not interested in revolt on this issue: "But for me, I live in the world as it is today, with its standards of beauty and its social customs."

Marjorie McGowan makes the task seem insuperable and even quixotic: "But one look at the radiance of movie stars in their middle forties, achieved solely through a higher standard of living and the alchemy of the modern beauty temples, is enough to convince millions of women that this is something they want too. Who, we may ask, is Jack Bustelo to leave us with the implication that this is something ridiculous?"

(But doesn't the struggle against Jim Crow involve breaking down the Nazi-like racial standard of beauty in Hollywood? Is that ridiculous?)

On this question I think E. Patrick of Los Angeles was dead right when she pointed in the *Militant* to the working-class women for leadership in this battle as well as on other fronts of the struggle for socialism. Referring to women's "present adherence to bourgeois society" as indicated "by their devotion to the standards of beauty of the ruling class," she is of the opinion that "working-class women, like the working class generally, are abandoning these bourgeois standards." This may be stated too strongly but it is certainly correct insofar as the whole direction of development tends in that direction. We can confidently expect women of the revolutionary socialist movement to transcend bourgeois standards and give leadership as Marxists on this important ideological front.

And we may be sure that they will find allies among the petty-bourgeois women—yes, even among the movie stars made radiant by the alchemy of Hollywood. Does that sound farfetched? Let us listen to an expert of the question, Gloria Swanson, who, born March 27, 1899, still looks radiant at the age of fifty-five.

Her testimony at the same time offers us an opportunity to check some of our conclusions about cosmetics with the virtual rigor of a laboratory control, since she isn't even faintly aware of our discussion; and, in addition, approaches the whole question not from the basis of beauty but of morality.

The necessity to lie

In an article in the September 26 issue of *This Week*, she discusses the question, "Should a woman lie about her age?"

"I can work up a full head of steam about the entire subject, which I feel is a tip-off on a sad state of affairs existing these days," the noted actress says. "I mean simply this: Nearly every woman in America develops a strong consciousness of age when the 30th milestone looms on the horizon." From then on nearly every woman begins to lie about her age.

Gloria Swanson very correctly expresses her indignation at those men who "stand snickering on the sidelines." But lying about her age is not the fault of the women. "A woman, you see, would never stoop to lying about her age if the men of America didn't put such a premium on youth. We are without doubt the most age-conscious country in the world and the male has set the pace. *The masculine point of view makes a woman feel that age is some sort of contagious disease or a dirty word."* (Miss Swanson's emphasis.)

Then she strikes hard: "Our shallow men go gaga about screen stars who only yesterday—in some cases quite literally—played hopscotch on the corner after school. They crane their necks to ogle the bikini-clad saplings on the beaches and dig each other in the ribs as they nod in the direction of the new office girl, overdressed, overbearing and under twenty."

And so the older women try to keep up by snipping off the years. Is this moral? Here Gloria Swanson adopts a viewpoint that a Marxist must agree corresponds with proletarian morality: "I am convinced that a woman is justified in fibbing if her livelihood and happiness, as well as those of her family, are at stake. But only then."

Where a competent woman might be denied a job because of her age, this defender of women's rights does "not hesitate one moment" to advise: "Give the prospective employer any age you can reasonably get away with. If he's so foolish as to set an arbitrary limit, ignoring experience and proved ability, he deserves to be lied to. Besides, you must look out for yourself and your family."

It is perfectly evident that Gloria Swanson's approach on this point parallels that of a Marxist—if economic necessity compels you to lie about your age of course you lie. (The form of the lie, whether a phony employment record or use of cosmetics is not important here.)

But does this economic necessity hold as an absolute? Shall we convert it into an aesthetic necessity? No, says Gloria Swanson. "This reasoning, I believe, is perfectly sound when self-protection is genuinely and seriously involved. But in all other circumstances, I can see no real point in camouflage."

Her grounds for this reasoning deserve the attention of all of us:

"First, because deception about age only serves to abet

this silly glorification of youth.

"And second, whom are you kidding, anyway?"

That in my book rates as a principled stand on this question, showing that to some degree at least, Gloria Swanson has seen through some powerful fetishes.

Then she indicates that not all men fall in the category of "shallow." "Sociological studies have shown that there's a high degree of marital happiness when men (the more intelligent ones!) consider other qualities more important than age and marry women older than themselves." We would say this was an indication not so much of intelligence as of freedom from certain fetishes cultivated today under capitalism. This freedom from fetishism is sometimes accidental and in any case not in one-to-one ratio to intelligence.

To illustrate her point, Gloria Swanson tells about a girl who lied about her age and married a man who thought she was much younger. When he found out, he was hurt and angry. "Not because she was older than he thought (he, too, had some brains) but because she had lied to him. And if she held the truth lightly in one case, he thought, what was her character like in others."

This man, who sought character in his mate, was however intelligent enough to understand why she had lied and he had sufficient character himself "to forgive her."

In Gloria Swanson's opinion any man to whom a few years makes any difference "isn't worth marrying in the first place." She advises an older woman considering marriage with a younger man to tell him her age. "Let him know the facts. If it bothers him, let him go his merry way, chasing the young, clinging things who don't have the fascination of an older woman."

Finally, Gloria Swanson indicates what her norm is. "The Europeans have the right idea about these things. Over there, a woman isn't really interesting to a man until she is in her forties. The European male seeks more than a youthful figure and candy-box face. He wants some imagination, some sense, some of the essential fineness of mind and spirit that maturity brings to a woman.

"But over here it's different and it bothers the girls no end."

Thus from this former Hollywood star we learn that if economic necessity demands it, of course we lie about such things as our age and looks. But from any other viewpoint the camouflage is pointless and even vicious. After all, what really counts is character. Since the current American standard is seriously wrong, we must seek a better one. Gloria Swanson finds it in Europe, whereas a Marxist looks to the working class, but both can agree that there are many women today and at least some men who have reached the conclusion that things are not right.

Well, Gloria Swanson's article could stand some sharpening and modification from a Marxist point of view—she leaves out, for instance, the class struggle and its influence, and she underrates the maturity of some youth, overlooks their need for camouflage, and misses the special problems they face—but her article indicates that she for one thinks something might be done about the false standards "over here."

Is it really so daring to venture the opinion that there are other American women, especially in the working class, who will agree with her on that and begin doing something about breaking down the capitalist standards of beauty? Why shouldn't the Marxists stand in the forefront of such a development, offering it leadership and theoretical clarification, especially on the secret of the fetish of cosmetics that deludes both men and women?

3. An exchange on the origins of women's oppression

Letter on Evelyn Reed articles

Dear Comrades:

Enclosed is a document which I wish to submit for your consideration and for publication in a discussion bulletin.

The document requires a preface which I submit, also, in the form of this letter. You will, perhaps, be both unprepared and taken aback by the sharp, factional tone with which this document is written. This is neither accidental, nor does it have its beginnings here. Over a year ago, Comrade Reed and I engaged in an exchange of correspondence in which she was warned that her interpretations were false and that if she persisted along the lines of her thesis I would consider it my duty to expose her theories as incorrect. She has elected to continue and even had the temerity to publish in the magazine rather than in a discussion bulletin.

It may seem to some that the question under consideration is only an academic subject over which so much heat and sharpness is unwarranted. However, such is rarely the case when we are dealing with the underlying forces of life.

A correct interpretation of the primitive social forms and the forces which brought them into existence is in direct relation to their subsequent evolution; and most especially concerns us in their relation to the role of the family today and of the future. We cannot hope to correctly interpret the forces which underlie the family today, nor those which have determined the modern relation between the sexes, without a scientific knowledge and interpretation of their historic sub-structure, for today's family is only an historic continuation with its roots buried deep in our primitive and primeval past. It is to the past that the women must turn in seeking out the keys of their destiny, before they can with knowledge and certainty turn to the future.

The sharp tone employed in this document is not the result of any personal antipathy toward any individual. It arises irrepressibly out of my firm inner conviction that such interpretations of primitive society and primitive social forms as are current in the party today, and have been for the last seventy-five years or so, are not just accidentally false or innocently misguided. I feel they are an integral part of and the historic extension of the general current of sexual factionalism which is and has been rife in the revolutionary movement. This undercurrent of conflict and struggle which boils up on the slightest provocation is, in turn, only an extension of that which takes place throughout capitalist society as a whole. It will not be resolved until such time as the socialist world brings forth new generations of men and women into a culture which will permit each sex to develop its own capacities and potentialities to the fullest.

We live in a world in which the masculine values appear to have submerged the feminine values virtually into a state of obliteration, and the battered feminine ego must either accept ignominious effacement or seek restitution through a cheap and second-rate imitation of maleness. We, none of us, can function as whole women in today's society, and we wreak our vengeance on the men through destruction of the male personality in childhood and through inability to respond to and find delight in the complementary qualities of the opposite sex. Thus, in capitalist society, half-men and half-women glare at each other across an abyss at the bottom of which can be found the beaten spirits and destroyed personalities of the children—the future generation.

The socialist society will free the sexes. However, freedom is but the recognition of necessity. The male ego will find that it must move over and make room for that of the female, else the victory shall turn to ashes and the struggle not worth the effort. But this will not come about through wishing it, nor passing laws, nor a correct theoretical appraisal of the situation. It will come about, like everything else, in direct relation to the degree to which man gains control and mastery over his environment. Above all, it will come about as the communal world finally turns its attention to the needs of the immature human young and to the realization that with the child lies all of the hopes, all of the daring, all of the dreams, all of the future of the communist world.

In the young, pliable, eager, responsive minds of tomorrow's children lies the certain success of our communist future. The molding of each developing personality, with all of its vast potentialities and its essential human dignity, into patterns of self-fulfillment and happiness will be the most exalted task which can be performed in our communist future, and in the performance of this task women will come into their own.

I firmly believe that the women can look to the future with the certain knowledge that theirs will be a glorious position of dignity and human worth. But this position will never be achieved, nor do I believe that women in their vast majority will seek to achieve it, by the route current in the party today—through continued competition and conflict with the men. To conceive that this competition and conflict will be carried over into the communist world is to admit defeat of the historic aims of mankind—that of the happiness and the self-fulfillment of the individual. It means that all which is detestable between the sexes in the decadent society of today will be carried over into the new.

I, for one, see no such perspective for the communist society. Rather, this will be a world in which neither the male values nor the female values will monopolize the attention of the new culture, but will be as two opposite halves which together make a unified whole. And from the whole men and women of tomorrow will come the whole child, certain in his knowledge that he no longer lives in a hostile world but lives in one which considers him its most precious asset, and in an environment of love and consideration for him as an individual he will grow to maturity along with his millions of brothers and sisters. Thus, generation will succeed generation in which self-fulfillment of the individual male and female become the prime goal and motive force of life.

It will be clear from the brief outline of my views above that I differ seriously with the evaluations current in our movement on the woman question. The differences are not only deep going but of long standing. It is difficult, if not impossible, to maintain an objective, disinterested, and academic tone on a subject which bears a direct, even though not apparent, relation to our life today as women, and on which such serious differences exist.

This brief explanation accompanies my document and should be published as its preface.

Comradely yours,
Marjorie McGowan

Marjorie McGowan

A criticism of the Evelyn Reed articles on the subject of the primitive family

This criticism deals with some aspects of the Reed articles published in the Spring and Summer issues of *Fourth International.* At the outset, I wish to state that I believe it imperative that the editors of the magazine disassociate themselves from any possible suspicion of official sanction of these theories and make it clear to the public that these articles represent the opinions of Evelyn Reed, *alone,* and in no way represent an official position.

Possibly not one comrade in 100 within the party is capable of forming a critical judgement of the Reed articles through having made a comprehensive survey of the new source material involved. In spite of this obvious drawback to the formation of an official, or even of a personal opinion, some individuals have become virtually lyrical concerning the Reed articles and it is not inconceivable that a concerted move will be on foot to spend party funds for their publication in pamphlet form.

The comrades of the Political Committee and of the party

as a whole should be informed that these articles stand on a very low level of academic achievement and that any good bourgeois anthropologist could quite easily make short work of them. We make ourselves look ridiculous in the eyes of informed individuals in the bourgeois academic world by any official sponsorship of this scholastically irresponsible attempt at defining primitive social forms and the forces which brought them into existence. It will be clear from the brief criticism below that such is the case and it is to be hoped that steps will be taken to thwart any move for official sanction of these theories.

The main body of this criticism does not deal with Comrade Reed's first article entitled "The Myth of Women's Inferiority," which appeared in the Spring issue of the magazine. Much of this first article is given over to the enumeration of facts regarding the role of primitive women in relation to the evolution of primitive production.

There is nothing new in any of these facts. They have been set down time and again by able anthropologists and Reed has quoted most of the major authorities correctly enough. What *is* new in this listing of factual information is the historical context given to these facts by Reed. Her attempts at defining the social forms which flow out of primitive woman's role as producer, the role of the primitive male, and the dynamic relationship between the two, must pass the tests of scientific methodology, and in this she fails miserably.

It would take nothing short of a book to unravel the falsity of the sweeping generalizations by which she wrenches primitive woman, the producer, out of historic context, and erects a tower of theory regarding the general relation between the sexes from primitive society down to the present day. In this, also, there is nothing new. She has simply taken the old feminist empiricism, superficiality, and the preconceived theoretical baggage of "women's enslavement to the lecherous male" which has never solved the enigma of the "woman question" for it remains to this day nothing more that that—a "question"—and added to all of this old junk some theories of her own invention.

This is a charge which the author of this criticism can make without a twinge of compunction. Let the comrades be the judge of the value of her feminist generalizations regarding the *general* relationship between the sexes throughout the whole of history found in her first article, when we inspect the content and the method used by Reed in her second article entitled "Sex and Labor in Primitive Society" in which she deals with the *specific* relation between the sexes of primitive society.

Comrades trained in the dialectic should react with a conditioned reflex of suspicion and wariness when confronted with any attempt at reducing highly complex social forces and relationships to a handful of criteria, all neatly and formally catalogued into convenient lists of A's, B's, and C's. Indicative of Reed's method is just such an attempt at the start of her second article, "Sex and Labor in Primitive Society," in the Summer issue of *Fourth International*. Even to many comrades uninformed on this subject, the attempt to reduce to formal classification the differences between the matriarchal and the patriarchal cultures should quite properly arouse mental reservations that such is not the method of the social scientist, regardless of the subject under investigation. Since it is necessary that we keep Reed's formal classifications freshly in mind during this brief criticism, we will quote them below for purposes of easy reference:

What are the outstanding characteristics of patriarchal society? Men play the dominant role in the labor process. Private property and class differentiation exist. The sex partners live together as man and wife under one roof, and are by law united in marriage. Fathers stand at the head of the family. The family is composed of father, mother (or mothers), and their children, and is the basic unit of society, through which property is inherited and passed on. These characteristics of the patriarchy are all features of *class society.*

In the matriarchy, on the other hand, women, not men, predominated in the labor process. There was no private ownership of community wealth. The sex partners did not live together under one roof—in fact, they did not even live in the same camp or compound. Marriage did not exist. Fathers did not stand at the head of the family because fathers, as fathers, were unknown. The elementary social group was composed exclusively of mothers and children—and for this reason has aptly been termed the "uterine family." Finally, the basic unit of society was not this uterine family of mothers and offspring, but the whole group, clan, or tribe. These characteristics of the matriarchy are all features of *primitive society,* which is sometimes described as "primitive communism" and is generally conceded to have preceded class society in the historical development of mankind ("Sex and Labor in Primitive Society," p. 85).

The uninitiated and innocent student who embarks on an exploration of primitive social forms armed with this blueprint will quite rapidly and unaccountably find himself bogged down in a quagmire of contradiction and confusion. Let us take, as two opposite and perhaps the most extreme, examples out of hundreds which could be selected: the case of Ancient Egypt versus the culture of the Australian aborigines, and attempt to fit them into the Reed pigeonholes.

Ancient Egypt was a matriarchy. Robert Briffault quotes the following authorities:

"The constitution of Egyptian society and of the family was characterized, says Dr. H.R. Hall, by 'a distinct preservation of matriarchy, the prominent position of women, and a comparative promiscuity in sexual relations.' 'Foremost in importance among the distinctive features of the social organisation,' says Professor Mitteis, 'was the position of women; Egypt from time immemorial was a land of matriarchal right'" (*The Mothers*, vol. 1, p. 379).

Matrilineal descent (i.e., descent through the mother) was the rule. Briffault says: "Descent was reckoned through the mother and not through the father" (ibid.)

Matrilocal residence prevailed. Briffault says:

> Marriage was matrilocal. Where there were two wives, each remained in her own home, the husband visiting them in turn. Not infrequently, especially in the Theban district, there was no cohabitation; both husband and wife remained in their respective homes. . . . All landed and house property was in the hands of the women; if a man built or acquired a house, it passed immediately to his wife. . . . The women, whether married or single, administered their property personally; the husband was not consulted and was generally ignorant of his wife's affairs. . . . Marriage does not appear to have been associated with any religious ceremony. It was essentially an economic transaction (ibid., p. 381–82).

Matriarchal Egypt, which produced a dazzlingly high civilization, can in no instance be called a "primitive society." Private property and class differentiation existed in its most vicious form—that of slave labor. The family was composed of mothers, fathers, and children, and was the basic unit of society, but the property was inherited and passed on through the female line. Fathers did not stand at the head of the family in this matriarchy, but fathers, as fathers, were known. It didn't really matter whether they were known or not known, since there were no illegitimate children in Ancient Egypt (ibid., p. 380). Briffault relates how the Greeks made merry over the henpecked husbands of Egypt.

Clearly, Ancient Egypt doesn't fit, no matter how hard we might squeeze and wriggle it around, into the Reed categorical imperative. And Ancient Egypt cannot be dismissed as simply a minor exception to the rule since many of the keys to the dynamism of the Mediterranean development must be sought in this venerable and brilliant civilization.

When we turn to the culture of the Australian aborigines, an even more extraordinary mass of contradiction appears. We must give the term "patriarchy" to the Australian social order, but only for want of a better term. A patriarchal relationship of forces between the sexes exists among the Australians, but due to the association of this term with a higher level of culture among those who must fit all phenomenon into formal classifications, the term is somewhat misleading.

Among the Australians, evidence of the existence of a former matriarchal order exists in abundance. Briffault says:

"Australian aboriginal society is, in fact, more patriarchal in character than many that are in a far higher stage of cultural and social development, and it is only owing to its low culture and isolation that the patriarchal social system and the patriarchal family have not entirely supplanted amongst them the primitive organization of maternal clans" (ibid., p. 727).

Descent may be either matrilineal or patrilineal, but far and away the greater number of clans trace descent through the mother, and the maternal totemic clan system is remarkable for its complexity. Robert Lowie says:

"Of the Australians some tribes are matrilineal, others patrilineal, but the lot of woman is not one jot better or more dignified among the former" (*Primitive Society*, p. 189).

Marriage is, by and large, patrilocal. Lowie says: "The Australians are patrilocal, at least often in the sense that a woman removes to her husband's band" (ibid., p. 161).

Briffault says: "Among the Australian tribes . . . the general rule, so far as recent observation goes, is for the husband to take his wife home to his own tribe, and nowhere, as has been seen, is the condition of women more degraded and oppressed" (*The Mothers*, vol. 1, p. 337). Speaking of the position of women, Briffault says:

> Among the Australian aborigines the condition of the women is utterly degraded. "Nowhere else," remarks a resident of long standing amongst them, "is it possible to meet with more miserable and degraded specimens of humanity than the women of Australia. The women are treated by the men with savage brutality."
>
> "The woman's life is of no account if her husband chooses to destroy it, and no one ever attempts to protect her or take her part under any circumstances. In times of scarcity of food she is the last to be fed and is not considered in any way." . . . "Blows over the head with a stick are the more common modes of correction, and spearing through the body for a slight offence." . . . "Few women," says Byre, "will be found upon examination to be free from frightful scars upon the head or the marks of spear wounds about the body."

And to this Briffault adds:

> Female Australian skulls commonly show, in fact, huge scars from old fractures. Any female, old or young, found unprotected is almost invariably ravished, and in most instances killed afterwards. Queensland natives chastise their wives by rubbing hot coals over stomachs. A central Australian native, being annoyed with his wife, was with difficulty dissuaded by some missionaries from roasting her alive over a slow fire (ibid., pp. 311–13).

Clearly, in this culture, fathers stand at the head of the family. Is this a consequence of knowledge of paternity? Briffault says:

"The tribes of Central Australia so carefully studied in the classical investigations of Sir Baldwin Spencer and Mr. Gillen were stated by them not to recognise any relation between sexual congress and reproduction, and the suggestion that there exists any such relation is, when made to those natives, received with derision . . . The accuracy of the report appears to be now fully established" (ibid., vol. 2, p. 446).

Paternity, it must be noted here, among most primitive tribes is not a physiological relation, but a sociological one. Lowie says:

"Biological paternity is one thing, sociological fatherhood another. The polyandrous Toda (an Australian group) do not trouble themselves about the former but establish the latter by a purely conventional rite" (*Primitive Society*, p. 167).

And Briffault: "The notion of paternity was not generally regarded in ancient and modern times, and is not regarded by the majority of primitive peoples, as representing a physiological relation, but a social and juridic claim. A father is 'responsible' for a woman's child in the economic and juridic sense" (*The Mothers*, vol. 2, p. 445).

Clearly, the ascendancy of the males in Australian culture is not the product of their knowledge of fatherhood, "as fatherhood." Is it then the result of a revolution in primitive economics? Quite the contrary, the Australians reside on a very low level of primitive culture and there exists no private ownership of communal wealth. Briffault quotes Mr. Taplin:

"'In the clan (of the Australians) there can be no personal property . . . all implements, weapons, etc., belong to the tribe collectively; every individual regards them as possessions of his clan, and to be employed for its welfare and defense as occasion may require.' And further on:

"An individual has no personal rights to game, fish or vegetable food he may obtain" (ibid., p. 493).

Briffault maintains that the patriarchal character of these primitive tribes is due to the unique circumstances in which their development took place, i.e., their isolation on the Australian continent. This, it must be maintained, is only begging the question. No small number of primitive tribes live in isolation and under conditions of supreme backwardness and wretched conditions, but have maintained a matriarchal character. Furthermore, Australia is not the only culture in which women hold an abysmally low position among primitives. In Melanesia, in Fiji, and in parts of Africa similar conditions prevail. Briffault says:

"In some parts of Africa things are as bad. The Bangala of the Congo do quite commonly eat their wives. Not longer since than the year 1887 a Bangala chief cooly informed a missionary that he had eaten seven of his wives, and that he had invited their relatives to the feast in order that there should be no family unpleasantness" (ibid., vol. 1, p. 315).

The isolation involved, or the lack of it, provides the external setting in which the development took place. It in no way defines for us the human forces which brought into existence the patriarchal relationships of primitive Australia, nor does it define the human forces which account for the matriarchal form in Ancient Egypt coexisting with a class society in a high state of civilization.

The Reed method, foreign and repugnant to Marxist ideology, finds its author in difficulties at the start. The development of her subsequent theory is a veritable masterpiece of sleight-of-hand tricks designed to somehow or other squeeze the facts into the predesigned mold of the theory. This is accomplished, finally, by the simple technique of throwing out or ignoring all of the facts which contradict the theory and only mentioning those which appear to support it. No one could read even a small portion of the massive accumulation of new facts involved in any discussion of primitive social forms and the course of their development without reaching the conclusion that in the Reed articles is a deliberate distortion of the facts, and deliberate omission of them, resulting in a totally perverted picture of primitive society.

It will be clear to the reader that both Comrade Reed and the author of this document refer extensively to Robert Briffault's monumental work, *The Mothers*. Reed, in her articles, has taken Briffault's conclusions on the matriarchal theory of social origins and has adapted them to some conclusions of her own regarding a "labor collective" and the primitive sexual relation. Her dishonesty lies in this: that what contradictions and discrepancies might appear in Briffault's conclusions as to the matriarchal character of our social origins arise out of the fact that he, as an honest scholar and researcher, *has set down all of the facts as he found them.* He did not resort to wishing them away or omitting them, and the contradictions between his massive accumulation of facts and his theory are there for all who have the eyes to see. Reed, on the other hand, resorts to what is known in psychology as wish fulfillment. Are the facts contradictory? Away with them! Let us fulfill the wish regardless of the facts! It could only have been in the interests of sexual factionalism that Reed has presented to an uninformed audience—her comrades in the SWP—such an utterly distorted and untruthful interpretation of the facts.

She says: "Under this totemic (or kinship) system, humanity was divided into two categories: kindred and strangers. All who were members of one totemic group were kin; all others were strangers" ("Sex and Labor," p. 88). (Once again, formal divisions and categories!) She then goes on to elaborate that the brothers and sisters of the "labor collective" had to find their sex partners among the strangers and since the strangers were identified with the enemies, we find that "the very strangers who were sex-mates of the women were at the same time enemies to the brothers of these women. That is, the brothers of Group A fought the sex-mates of their sisters in Group B" (ibid.). And she goes on to quote Briffault at length that since the members of an outside group are the "enemies," and a state of warfare exists between clans, "it is quite impossible," says Briffault, "for a man to visit or hold any intercourse with another clan without running almost certain risk of being murdered" (ibid., p. 89).

Reed then goes on to sketch out a lurid picture on the basis of this quotation torn out of context, of sexual anarchy prevailing outside the clan, in which mating takes place only in secrecy and in "no-man's-land" outside the limits of the compound, with the relationship of the sex-mates confined to sexual union; socially they were strangers to each other. The "husbands and wives" did not live under the same roof, nor in the same compound or area; they did not provide for each other, and that between them existed a deep social gulf (ibid.).

Incredible as it may seem, this entire picture is a creation of Reed's fertile imagination. Briffault, her own authority, gives us no such intimation of anarchy in sexual relations in clans where the rule of exogamy is in force. (Exogamy, incidentally, is not universal. There are endogamous tribes at a low level of culture in which marriage and the sexual relation takes place within the clan.) Rather, Briffault goes on to point out the actual state of things which Reed chose to ignore:

> There is in nearly all the surviving examples of such societies (i.e., exogamous) an understanding whereby the members of a given group obtain their sexual partners from some other particular group, or groups, the members of which have intermarried with their own for generations. To marry into a totally strange group, between which and the group of the suitor there exists

no established custom of intermarriage and no understanding in this respect, is an unusual and difficult pro-
cedure. Those elaborate tribal conferences, negotiations,
diplomatic parleys and conciliatory exchanges of pres-
ents which have been noted in Australia, Melanesia, or
Polynesia, do not, of course, take place on the occasion
of every marriage; but they are necessary in the case
of the marriage of members of two different tribes between whom a regular practice of intermarriage has not
already become established. A man cannot marry into
a strange group without an agreement being concluded
by the two groups which will permit of intermarriage
between their members. Those negotiations and that
agreement have reference secondarily and incidentally
only to the particular individuals concerned; it is not the
relation between those individuals, but the relation between the two groups which is considered and discussed.
The contract, if concluded, is not an individual contract,
but a group-contract, and will permit of further intermarriage between members of the two groups without
the necessity of new negotiations. The considerations affecting the relations between the groups, and not those
between given individuals, are paramount, and are the
object of the transaction, the formal diplomatic and
juridical character of the proceedings have reference to
the former and not to the latter. Marriage in the most
advanced societies has preserved that character; it is a
formal juridic transaction. But that juridical character
had not originally reference to the relations established
between the man and the woman, but to the relations
between the groups to which they respectively belong.
In the ideas of more advanced phases of society the direct
purpose of the contract is to legalize the relation between
the man and the woman, giving it a juridic sanction, and
thus distinguishing it from "illegitimate" sexual relations.

But such is not quite the original character and purpose of the juridic transaction; its prototype is the agreement whereby intermarriage is rendered possible between the members of the groups. Such a contract is, in the most rudimentary and primitive human societies, a primary necessity if the rules against incest are to be observed; and it must of necessity have been the first "institution" or juridic regulation, or marriage. The original purpose of the institution of marriage, was thus quite other than the regulation of sexual relations or the safeguarding of claims of individual possession. It had not reference to individuals, but to collective groups; it was not an individual marriage contract, but a group-marriage contract (*The Mothers*, vol. 1, pp. 562–63).

These two intermarriage groups, therefore, were not normally the enemies and in a state of perpetual warfare with each other, as Reed would have us believe. Quite the contrary, the group-marriage contract which prevailed between the two (or more) groups was the basis for the strongest social and juridic ties. Robert Lowie says:

A striking feature of the moieties (dual organization of exogamous clans) is the development of reciprocal services. At an Iroquois burial the functionaries are always selected not from the deceased person's but from the opposite moiety, and the same holds for the remote Cahuilla of southern California. On the coast of northern British Columbia certain festivals are never arranged except in honor of the complementary moiety. . . . Other functions of moieties have already been cited. Those of the Iroquois are characteristic of the Eastern Indians. At such games as lacrosse members of opposite moieties are pitted against each other. At feasts and ceremonies there is a corresponding spatial grouping; one moiety faces the other, each being represented by a speaker (*Primitive Society*, pp. 133–34).

The principle of sexual separation laid down by Comrade Reed as an immutable law of social unification becomes, in fact, transformed into its opposite when we deal with the larger social body. *Sexual unification* is the only possible basis for *social unification* of two otherwise warring and antagonistic units of primitive society, and the sexual relation, far from being the prime disrupter and disorganizer of all primitive human relations, is the very cement and bond holding together the larger social group. All generalizations are dangerous regarding primitive society if they do not account for all of the facts, as they rarely do, but no generalization is perhaps safer than that *sexual separation, or the rule of exogamy, within a group is only achieved through sexual unification with some other group or groups.* Under the conditions of primitive society, given the heterogeneous and antagonistic character of the diverse groups and the miles of hostile wilderness which may separate them, no group could long survive if the sexual relation was banned within the group and only sexual anarchy prevailed without.

The matriarchal form, far from being the self-sufficient and self-contained clan of Reed's invention is a *dual organization*. It is composed, in its simplest manifestation, of two parts, and it is impossible to consider or to understand the one part except in its relation to its opposite part—the group (or groups) with which it is "married" and which provides for the needs of reproduction. In the relationship of forces between these two parts of the organic whole are to be found all of the basic ingredients upon which civilization has been subsequently constructed. These dynamic relationships, needless to say, do not correspond all over the globe and at all stages of culture to Reed's formalistic and rigidly conceived "classic" matriarchal form composed of mothers, sisters, and brothers, with husbands excluded from all participation in the economic and social life of the clan into which they have married. Quite the contrary, the relationships between the two intermarriage groups are of the greatest variety and fluidity and anthropologists by the dozens have set down tons of facts indicating that no such formal schema as Reed's exists, and have attempted to find some sort of pattern and law which has governed the direction of development in this vast *diversity* of primitive relationships and primitive social forms. We can only say that Reed has acted in an irresponsible manner when she ignores the great wealth of new facts found in her own source material showing that *none of her absolute values or generalizations have any universal application whatsoever.*

It would seem, from reading the Reed articles, that primitive marriage, for instance, does not exist. In fact, she says so in her criteria on what constitutes a matriarchy. "Marriage," she says, "did not exist" ("Sex and Labor," p. 85). This is nothing short of incredible! Robert Briffault, her principle authority, has no less than two full columns in the index of *The Mothers,* vol. 3; no less than seventy index references to primitive marriage and includes some of the following references:

> marriage, attempts to define . . . often difficult to distinguish from irregular relations . . . not regarded as arising out of personal inclination . . . from love, condemned as immoral . . . not regarded as a private concern . . . regarded as a social institution . . . traditions of its institution . . . not distinguished from other sexual relations . . . distinguished from . . . rules of, primarily intended to avoid incest . . . economic, sexual and sentimental aspects . . . economic grounds for . . . arranged in infancy . . . by parents and others . . . consent of whole tribe or village required . . . acquiesced in by parties concerned . . .

contracted and celebrated by all members of respective families . . . agreement between two groups . . . group-marriage, between intermarriage classes, or fraternal sororal families . . . of cross-cousins . . . juridic conception of . . . not regarded as concluded before birth of child . . . stabilized by birth of children . . . not severed by wife's death . . . loose and unstable character of . . . lasts only as long as husband can provide adequate supply of food . . . temporary and trial . . . by service . . . associated with tests of endurance . . . by purchase, a commutation of marriage by service . . . (see *The Mothers*, vol. 3, p. 794).

These are only a few of the references found in Briffault's index. They refer to discussion, interpretation, and factual information on primitive marriage of from one to one hundred pages in length per reference. And Reed can say that "Marriage did not exist"!! To what purpose, Comrade Reed?

It would only be charitable to suggest that Reed may have been blinded into wishing the marriage relation away by the virtually unanimous verdict of anthropologists who testify to the instability of the individual marriage relation. However, Reed, who finds it quite easy to accept the principle of "social motherhood" and "social brotherhood" shows a singular blind spot when it comes to "social marital relations." While it is undeniably true in primitive society that the *individual* sexual and marriage relation is highly unstable, the *social* sexual and marriage relation, that is, the relation between two tribes who are "married" is of the greatest stability.

Thus, it is more common than not and, in fact, is virtually universal, to find that the adult males present in the maternal clan are precisely those husbands (whom Reed banishes away by enclosing the term in quotation marks) who perform all of the duties incumbent upon the adult males and which Reed claims can only be performed by desexed brothers—that is, the husbands are the providers of animal food and the protectors of the clan of their in-laws. While they may, with the greatest of frequency, change their sexual partners and their marital status within the group, this in no way affects their role as protectors and providers of animal food for the group as a whole. No matter to whom they are married at the moment, their loyalties and their duties apply to the entire group of in-laws as a whole in the clan with which their own clan has an intermarriage agreement.

The "husbands and wives," says Reed, did not provide for each other. "The relationship between sex-mates was confined exclusively to sexual union" ("Sex and Labor," p. 89). Another incredible product of Reed's imagination!

Robert Lowie says: "A Kai (for instance) does not marry because of desires he can readily gratify outside of wedlock without assuming any responsibilities; he marries because he needs a woman to make pots and to cook his meals, to manufacture nets and weed his plantations, in return for which he provides the household with game and fish and builds the dwelling" (*Primitive Society*, p. 66).

Throughout the whole of primitive society, it is axiomatic among anthropologists that the adult males do not marry to obtain sexual gratification, which can readily be obtained in most primitive groups outside of marriage. The male marries to obtain an economic associate, to have a woman who will cook, sew, and make life comfortable for him—just as the woman marries to obtain a provider and protector.

Briffault says: "Individual marriage has its foundation in economic relations. In the vast majority of uncultured societies, marriage is regarded almost exclusively in the light of economic considerations" (*The Mothers*, vol. 2, p. 1). He goes on:

> The answer of the Australian aborigines to the question why they desire a wife will bear repeating, for the purposes of primitive individual marriage could not be

more clearly and accurately stated. If a native is asked why he is anxious to possess a wife, he invariably answers, "to fetch me wood and water and prepare my 'mudlinna' (food)." . . . In the Pelew Islands "marriage is regarded as a matter of business, love is left to youth." . . . The same is true of all uncultured peoples. Among the natives of northern Papua 'a woman is acquired in the first place as a worker and only incidentally as a wife." . . .

With the Eskimo, "in a man's choice of a wife the feelings are not taken into account," he "marries because he requires a woman's help to prepare his skins, make his clothes, and so forth." "The marriage relation was entered upon from reasons of interest or convenience with very little regard for affection as we understand it." Among the North American Indians "industry and capacity for work are above all valued, and next fertility." . . . Among the Banyoro "marriages are seldom, if ever, the outcome of love, but are entered into for utilitarian and economic reasons" (ibid., pp. 164–66).

The considerations which determine primitive woman's choice of her mate, are, however, of the same practical nature as those which may influence a man's choice of a wife. Thus of the woman of the Sea Dayaks it is said that they "generally regard marriage as a means of obtaining a man to work for them"; and "a woman will often separate from her husband simply because he is lazy." Among the Eskimo a woman "appears to desire a husband who is industrious and a good hunter." "They cling to us," said an Eskimo, "because we give them food and clothing." When a hunter is sick, his wife goes to another. Skill in hunting and prowess in war is amongst all the North American tribes the chief recommendation in a prospective husband. "Natural affection," says the Rev. D. Jones, "seems very small. By women beauty is commonly no motive for marriage; the only inducement seems to be the reward which a man gives her." Among the tribes of Louisiana a woman's "only care is to inform herself whether he who asks her is an able hunter, a good warrior and an excellent workman." Among the Hidatsa "parents commonly advise their daughters to marry men who will never leave the lodge unprovided with meat." The advice appears, however, superfluous. The manner in which a Pennsylvanian Indian expressed the motives which influence the choice and the attachment of the American Indian woman could not be improved upon for terseness: "Squaw" he said, "loves to eat meat—no husband, no meat—so squaw do everything to please husband—he do same to please her—live happy" (ibid., pp. 181–82).

And Briffault goes on: "No primitive woman will willingly consent to marry a man who has not given proof of his functional fitness to perform his share in the economic division of labor which constitutes the marriage association." "The capacity to provide such samples of the hunter's skill is the indispensable prerequisite of individual marriage throughout primitive society" (ibid., pp. 183–84).

And Robert Lowie says: "Marriage, as we cannot too often or too vehemently insist is only to a limited extent based on sexual considerations. The primary motive, so far as the individual mates are concerned, is precisely the founding of a self-sufficient economic aggregate" (*Primitive Society*, pp. 65–66).

Wherefore, then, is Reed's "labor collective" composed solely of mothers, sisters, and brothers, with husbands excluded from all social and economic participation in the group and a relation between husbands and wives reduced exclusively to sexual union? Wherefore, is Reed's "motherhood-brotherhood" in clans where the "social brothers" show an unfortunate tendency to marry and settle down in the clan of their in-laws, as is true in the overwhelming majority of maternal clans with matrilocal residence. These husbands, far from causing the entire clan to fly apart through sexual conflict, are the principal providers of animal food and protectors of the clan, since the mature brothers of their wives have generally departed on a similar quest elsewhere. Far from being an exception to the rule, the marriage of individuals as an economic consideration—*and as an economic necessity—is absolutely universal in primitive societies, from the rudest hunting tribes to the most sophisticated,* and it is not unknown, although certainly not the rule, among the very rudest of cultures to find "matrimonial relations that would be rated exemplary by a mid-Victorian moralist. Among the Andaman Islanders 'conjugal fidelity' till death is not the exception but the rule" (ibid., p. 167).

The "classic" matriarchy, which Comrade Reed would have us believe is universally found at all levels of culture and is representative of primitive relations as a whole, far from being found at the lowest level of primitive society, is found almost exclusively at the higher levels of neolithic culture verging on civilization. And the examples of this "classic" matriarchy—of what a self-respecting matriarchy ought to look like—are few and far between, the Iroquois and the Pueblos being the examples, par excellence. However, even here, Reed has given us a distorted picture of the primitive sexual and marriage relation.

Among the Zuni, a Pueblo tribe, where a woman's authority is absolute, "When a man returns from his day's work his wife drops whatever work she may be doing and goes to the door of the house to greet him. Whatever he brings she takes from him and carries into the house. Then she sets out food for her husband. These gestures demanded by etiquette symbolize the economics of marriage. The house belongs to the woman and she receives her husband in it as a guest. He in turn brings the produce of the fields and ranch; as it crosses the threshold it becomes the property of the woman. Any omission of these formalities on the part of the woman would be interpreted by the man as an indication that she no longer regards him as her husband.

"The economic interdependence of men and women is one of the great stabilizing forces of family life. It does not prolong the life of any individual marriage but it helps to maintain the institution. The Zuni change mates frequently but man-woman-child constellation remains constant. There are no bachelors, spinsters, or abandoned children" (Boas and others, *General Anthropology*, p. 370).

And Briffault reports, speaking of the Zuni "In the living and cooking-room, round the wood-fire, the inmates might be seen sitting assembled in the evening . . . fathers, mothers and children. . . . Though the husband takes up his abode in the wife's family dwelling during her life and his good behavior, he belongs still to his own family . . . with the woman rests the security of the marriage ties; and it must be said, in her high honour, that she rarely abuses the privilege, that is, never sends her husband to the home of his father's unless he richly deserves it" (*The Mothers*, vol. 1, pp. 272–3). And continuing:

"The domestic life of the Zunis," says Mrs. Stevenson, "might well serve as an example for the civilized world. They do not have large families, and the members are deeply attached to one another. . . . The young mothers would be seen caring for their infants, or perhaps the fathers would be fondling them, for the Zuni men are very devoted to their children, especially the babies. The grandmother would have one of the younger children in her lap, with perhaps the head of another resting against her shoulder, while the rest would be sitting near or busying themselves about household matters." "The house," says Dr. Kroeber, "belongs to the women, born of the family. There they come into the world, pass their lives, and within the walls they die. As they grow up, their brothers leave them, each to abide in the house of his wife. (!) Each woman, too, has her husband, or succession of husbands, sharing her blankets. (!) So generation succeeds generation, the slow stream of mothers and daughters forming the current that carried with it husbands, sons and grandsons" (ibid., p. 273).

Even giving Reed all the benefits of the doubt and selecting as an example one of the most perfect cases of primitive matriarchal form extant, where, we may ask, is this supposed gulf between sexual partners as a universal criteria? Where, we may ask, is a sexual relation in which sedulous separation of the married couples must be maintained else all of primitive society would fly apart through sexual conflict of the adult males? Of separate abodes which must be maintained as a necessity, everywhere and always—when, as a matter of fact, sometimes it is and sometimes it isn't? Of a sexual relation which must take place in secrecy and in a "no-man's land" beyond the compounds for fear of detection by the "enemy"?

Even on this last statement, Briffault makes no such categorical statement as does Reed. He lists, in fact, the Tahitians, the Maori of New Zealand, the Eskimo, the Creeks, the tribes of New Mexico, the Potocudoes, the Indians of Paraguay, the Choroti of the Pilcomayo, the Negritos of the Andaman Islands, the Guegians, and the Australian aborigines, as being some of the tribes in which copulation quite normally and naturally takes place in public, before any observers who happen to be around including the relatives of the female participant, with the most complete indifference to any sense of indecency or fear (ibid., vol. 3, pp. 260–61).

And he goes on to point out that while privacy in the sexual relation is almost universally sought out and while it *can* be the effect of actual danger attending such relations at the hands of a man's in-laws, that "The privacy demanded remains, in fact, desirable chiefly for its own sake, and the main consideration in seeking it is the desire to be sheltered from all disturbing influences" (ibid., p. 262).

Where, in this brief review of some of the contradictions, discrepancies and unfounded generalizations of the Reed articles can we find evidence to support her sweeping statements that "under the totemic system a sexual gulf separated those who, as kinfolk, lived and worked together in the same totemic group or labor collective. Conversely, a social gulf separated those who, as strangers, were united sexually"?

On the contrary, *there exists no such mechanically contrived cleavage of sex and society in any primitive culture—from the most savage to the most civilized.* What contradiction and dualism exists lies in the fact that the sexual relation is at one and the same time the great divider and the great unifier of primitive social relations. Needless to say, this dualism in the relation of sex to society has far wider and more profound implications when we consider its origins and its application to the larger aspects of theory. The supporters of the matriarchal theory of social origins, and Comrade Reed in particular, must explain for us *how a dual organization such as is the matriarchal form could ever have arisen out of the animal world.* Even so archconservative and cautious an observer as Robert Lowie says: "we may reasonably doubt whether a dual organization is really the simplest for primitive man" (*Primitive Society*, p. 136). And, indeed, we may not only reasonably doubt, but we may find that when we attempt to bring such a dual organization out of the animal world we can only do so by route of a fantasy, outlined as follows:

In the days of long, long ago, an animal herd from which we are descended, composed of mothers, sisters, daughters, and sexually immature brothers and sons, which had advanced far enough along in consciousness to so label and comprehend these relationship-concepts, found it necessary to somehow or other retain the adult brothers and sons within the group for the purposes of protection and provision of animal food and for the purposes of founding a "labor collective."

Because the sexual relation is the great disrupter of the labor process going on within this animal herd, the animal "brothers and sons" were arbitrarily banned from the herd on reaching sexual maturity through being advised that the animal females within the group were their "social mothers" and "social sisters" and, therefore, taboo under the laws of incest.

We must assume that these adult male animals, "sons and brothers," simply roamed at large, taking sex and sustenance wherever they found it, excluded from all participation in the "labor collective" which was in the process of formation.

When it became apparent to the mothers and sisters that they could no longer do the job by themselves, they cast around for ways and means whereby the adult sons and brothers could be kept at home and, at the same time, sexually satisfied since we assume these male animals were not eunuchs.

The Reed solution to their dilemma is that the mothers and sisters, by what strange sorcery we know not, simply told their brothers and sons to stay home after this, and if they wanted to indulge in sexual intercourse, they would have to content themselves with whatever stray enemy happened to pass by. To which, forthwith, the obedient animal sons obliged—and there they have been ever since, assisting in the construction of the "labor collective."

The solution to their dilemma, according to Robert Briffault and other supporters of the matriarchal theory, goes something as follows: the mothers and sisters looked around for some other herd in the same fix and between the two of them they thrashed out this burning problem on which the fate of humanity depended.

Thus it was, that a "founding convention of humanity" was called, the purpose of which was to unite two otherwise warring animal groups. The tendency of the adult males to squabble over the female is overcome by a juridical arrangement that each of these two herds shall henceforth provide for the sexual needs of the other in order that the adult male animals, who are forthwith transformed into "social brothers" can stay at home and help their moms. We must further assume that at this primordial "founding convention" the adult males were disenfranchised by their mothers and sisters, since we cannot conceive of a male animal making rules which will in the future regulate his sexual life to his own disadvantage. At any rate, since they hadn't been invited in yet, they were probably still roaming at large, unaware that their destiny was being taken into hand.

And so it is that the human race ceases to be animal and becomes human by a convention decree regulating sex in which one-half of the human race, the men, were excluded from participation and probably didn't even have a consultative vote. Since there must have been at least as many independent origins of mankind as there are races, this absurd conception is advanced by the supporters of the matriarchal theory as having occurred not once, but at least five times. And so, we have the picture well in mind of the primeval mothers, two-by-two, launching the male animal onto the ark of human experience.

We do not mean to sound fresh, but the entire conception is so preposterous that the temptation to succumb to sarcasm cannot be contained. Comrade Reed can erect a tower of theory on the basis of a supposed vast gulf and irreconcilability between sex and society *only so long as she omits the facts.* With the inclusion of the facts, a quite different

perspective on the origins and the evolution of the matriarchy is possible. It becomes clear, in fact, that the matriarchal form could not have been the most primitive, but was
preceded by a far more primal, now extinct form, of which
it was the negation.

Letter to Marjorie McGowan

Dear Comrade McGowan:

At its last meeting, the Political Committee considered your letter and your request that the editors of the magazine dissociate themselves from the position taken in the articles by Evelyn Reed.

The Political Committee felt it unnecessary to take a position either for or against Comrade Reed's articles. On such subjects the feeling was that considerable latitude is permissible so long as the author defends the materialist viewpoint, advocates and tries to apply the dialectic method, and seeks to supply material of an educational character (facts, presentation of various theories that try to account for them, etc.).

Within such a framework there is room for differences of opinion as to how successful the author was in achieving these objectives. From this standpoint, the editors were entirely correct in publishing the Reed articles.

Comradely yours,
Farrell Dobbs
NATIONAL SECRETARY

Evelyn Reed

Anthropology: Marxist or bourgeois?

A reply to Comrade McGowan

Comrade McGowan launches her attack against me on the following propositions:

(1) The "interpretations of primitive society and primitive social forms as are current in the party today, and have been for the last seventy-five years or so, are . . . false . . . or misguided." Even worse, these interpretations are not just "accidently" false or "innocently" misguided. Evidently we have been deliberately misled.

In this respect, I know of only one interpretation of primitive society which has been current in the party for the last seventy-five years or so, and which, indeed, we have openly embraced. This is the *Marxist* interpretation, as it was set down by Engels in his *Origin of the Family, Private Property and the State.*[14] I would like to hear further on this point from Comrade McGowan, since my own studies are based upon the work of Engels.

(2) Reed's "articles stand on a very low level of academic achievement and . . . any good bourgeois anthropologist

could quite easily make short work of them." Even worse, "we make ourselves look ridiculous in the eyes of informed individuals in the bourgeois world by . . . this scholastically irresponsible attempt at defining primitive social forms and the forces which brought them into existence."

I must confess that I did not set forth my propositions in the articles as an "academic achievement," "low" or otherwise. I set them forth as Marxist contributions which, in some points, are opposed to the academicians. Marxist contributions of any kind and on any score, are always considered "low" by certain bourgeois academicians. Nor did I concern myself with appearing ridiculous in the eyes of bourgeois "informed individuals." On the contrary, these informed individuals appear ridiculous to me, since they are unable to answer questions on subjects that they are supposed to be best informed about. They have left the *answering* of these questions to the "uninformed" Marxists.

Finally, my study is not *scholastic*, irresponsible or otherwise. On the contrary, scholastic individuals are terrified at the very thought of embarking upon my road of investigation, for this would soon expose the fact that modern bourgeois society represents only a fragment of time in human history and even that fragment is reaching the end of its road. Only the Marxists, who are polar opposites of scholastics, can look fearlessly into the past, because they can look fearlessly into the future and prepare for a socialist society.

(3) Reed attempts to "reduce to formal classification the differences between the matriarchal and the patriarchal cultures."

Comrade McGowan evidently did not read my article very carefully, or did not understand it. I was not "reducing this subject to formal classifications," whatever that means. I was declaring flatly that there was a *historical sequence* of these two social forms, and that the matriarchy came first in this historical sequence.

What is Comrade McGowan's position on this decisive question? I have searched very carefully for her position on this score, but can find only a cryptic reference to it in the very last sentence of her presentation, as follows: "It becomes clear, in fact, that the matriarchal form could not have been the most primitive, but was preceded by a far more primal, now extinct form, of which it was the negation."

What exactly does this sentence mean, Comrade McGowan? All I can deduce from it is that if the "more primal" or *first* form was not the matriarchal form, you have rejected Briffault's theory and stand on the side of his opponents. His opponents declare that the patriarchal form goes all the way back to the animal kingdom. Once we leave the animal kingdom, we can discuss only two *social* forms: the matriarchal and patriarchal. Regarding the central question of *which came first*—on which side do you stand?

For the benefit of those comrades who are unfamiliar with the big debate around this question, let me briefly explain its implications. The bourgeois anthropologists are not in agreement among themselves on many points. But the most fundamental difference is represented in this matriarchal-patriarchal debate. In fact, the position of each anthropologist on this question determines which of the two main schools of thought he belongs to and is a guide to his aims and methods.

One school adheres to the materialist and historical method of analyzing the anthropological data, even if only in limited or partial form. The other school is hostile to the historical method and substitutes for it mere fact-finding accompanied by impressionistic and superficial interpretations of these facts. The one school, therefore, is progressive and leads forward; the other is obscurantist and reactionary.

We do not stand on the sidelines in this matter. We support the materialist school, as Engels did when he supported Lewis Morgan and polemicized against Edward Westermarck.[15] We may, and do, use the findings of all schools, but we are extremely selective and highly critical when it comes to embracing interpretations and theories.

In the matriarchy-patriarchy debate, there are two opposing theories on the question of which came first. Edward Westermarck is perhaps the most explicit and authoritative spokesman for the position that the patriarchal system of marriage and family relations goes all the way back to the animal kingdom. His theory may be summed up in the popular picture of the ape "patriarch" who provides for and domineers over his "harem" of wives and offspring exactly as the patriarchal father in class society. As for the matriarchy, it never existed. Or, if it did exist, it was only a kind of social aberration found here and there on the sidelines of history.

Robert Briffault is the foremost exponent of the opposite position and in fact has set forth his proposition as "the matriarchal theory of social origins." All those who support Briffault, therefore, are declaring themselves on the side of the position that the matriarchy came first.

The Marxists are vitally concerned with this debate for the following reasons: the bourgeois myth that class society existed for all time and will continue to exist for all time is an obstacle in our path. We declare just the opposite: that class society is only a transient stage of human history, which arose at a certain historical juncture for certain specific reasons and will disappear at the next historical juncture for other specific reasons.

This bourgeois myth about the permanent fixture of class society is upheld and reinforced through the myth that the institutions of marriage and the family are also permanent fixtures. The Westermarckian theory, indeed, makes the modern social institutions of marriage and the family virtually a biological law that goes all the way back to the animal kingdom. Those two myths regarding class society and its marriage institution act as a kind of pincers by which the working people are held in ignorance, superstition, and subjugation. Our task is to demolish *both* aspects of this bourgeois myth.

Two great bourgeois theoreticians have prepared the groundwork for us in this big task of demolition. These are Lewis Morgan and Robert Briffault. Engels utilized Morgan's findings to demonstrate that before class society came into existence there was an earlier social system which he called "primitive communism." But as the science of anthropology developed, new terms came into existence, and the full meaning of these terms was not always immediately apparent. Thus, as I have tried to point out, the term "matriarchy" represents an equivalent term for "primitive communism," but this information is not widely disseminated. Discussions on the matriarchy usually center around its marriage form, called "matrilocal marriage," rather than on its economic and social structure which was primitive communistic. This has created a big smokescreen of heated debates on marriage forms, and has derailed the subject from its economic and class base.

To declare oneself on the side of the matriarchy as the earlier form of social organization, therefore, is to openly or implicitly declare oneself in agreement with the theory that primitive socialism or communism preceded class society. And that is the rub. To declare that primitive communism preceded class society is to admit that class society did not always exist and by the same token will not always exist. It is, in effect, to support the Marxist position and theory. And what bourgeois scientist who values his professorial chair will make such an admission?

All this is concealed behind the debate on matriarchy-patriarchy. It involves a question of class struggle and class ideology. That is why, out of the whole field of bourgeois scientists in anthropology over the past century, we have embraced the theories of only two: Morgan and Briffault. And it is noteworthy that both were subjected to intimidation, attack, and even partially suppressed. Today, under the pressure of bourgeois reaction and propaganda, to support these scientists is almost equivalent to supporting the Marxists and being classified as a "commie."

Apart from these two great theoreticians who dealt with social history, there is a great body of anthropological investigators, scholars, fact finders, and interpreters whose work, as important as it is, cannot be accepted uncritically. Even among these "reputable" scientists, there is a division, although it is more muffled and more difficult to discern. On the one hand, there are those who search for roots and causes, which involves the historical approach even on a limited scale. These are represented by such giant figures as Sir James Frazer, Robertson Smith, Lorimer Fison and A.W. Howitt, Baldwin Spencer and F.J. Gillen, W.H.R. Rivers, Andrew Lang, Hutton Webster, and a number of others. They were motivated primarily by scientific interest rather than the need to uphold class society and class prejudice.

On the other hand there is the modern superficial and impressionistic school of anthropologists, who are as much concerned with upholding bourgeois institutions as they are with science. Representatives of this school are Franz Boas, A.R. Radcliffe-Brown, Bronislaw Malinowski, R.H. Lowie, Alexander Goldenweiser, and a host of others, as well as the popularizers, such as Margaret Mead and Ruth Benedict.

The favorite theory of the impressionistic school of anthropologists is that society is a "diversity of cultures." This is certainly true. But it is no substitute for probing into social history and explaining the *evolution* of human society as it advanced through the ages. It is like pointing out that all human beings are somewhat different from each other, no two being exactly alike, as a substitute for declaring flatly that all human beings belong to the species Homo sapiens

Union women participating in 1978 march for the Equal Rights Amendment

and that this species had a million-year history beginning with the animal kingdom.

Against my preoccupation with the *history* of social forms, Comrade McGowan writes: "Anthropologists by the dozens have set down tons of facts . . . to find some sort of pattern and law which has governed the direction and development in this vast *diversity* (her emphasis) of primitive relationships and primitive social forms." Evidently it is this impressionistic and reactionary school of anthropologists that Comrade McGowan supports, for nowhere do I find any description of the "laws" governing primitive social forms. All I find is a bulky array of quotations, with no reference to their historical sequence, to prove merely the "diversity" of marriage and social forms.

This is simply applying the argument of the "diversity of cultures" school of anthropologists. According to their theory, since both matrilocal and patrilocal marriage forms are found in the relics of primitive groups, all you have to do is pay your money and take your choice. This is like saying that because there are still relics today of feudalistic and even slave class relations, there was no historical sequence of chattel slavery, feudalism, and capitalism; that all we have is merely a "diversity of forms."

If Comrade McGowan agrees with the antihistorical school of anthropologists and has dumped Briffault, it is incumbent upon her to come out openly and say so. Instead, she mixes up quotations from Briffault with quotations from his opponents to give the impression that they were all in agreement. The fact is, Briffault was *opposed* to the antihistorical school and I am in agreement with Briffault.

The great bulk of Comrade McGowan's presentation is devoted to making two main points: (1) Marriage is "universal." (2) "Economic considerations" governed marriage in both the matrilocal and patrilocal forms. Neither of these two points has anything whatever to do with the great debate on matriarchy-patriarchy. Thus Comrade McGowan is using the same techniques and methods as the school she supports to divert the discussion and obscure the issues.

Regarding the first point, of course marriage is "universal" in the same way and to the same degree that class society conquered primitive communism (or the matriarchy) and became the universal social system.

Regarding the second point, of course "economic considerations" governed ancient marriage forms. The fact is, economic considerations have governed marriage from its first form, matrilocal marriage, to its last form, modern capitalist marriage or monogamy.

But what have these points got to do with the question at hand, namely, *which form of marriage came first historically?* Briffault left no ambiguity on this score. The reason why he centered so much of his attention upon matrilocal marriage was precisely to demonstrate that it was the *universal form of marriage* before patrilocal marriage came into existence. He was dealing with the question from the standpoint of historical sequence, and not from the standpoint of demonstrating any "diversity" of cultures or marriage.

There are three main forms of marriage historically; the first was matrilocal marriage which is associated with the matriarchy; the second was patrilocal marriage, associated with the patriarchy; and the final, most complete form, is monogamy which is the form we know. It took Briffault twenty years to amass the material on the universality of the matrilocal form of marriage as the earliest form, and with it he knocked the props out of the Westermarckian theory of the permanence of the marriage institution. This did not prevent a whole school of Westermarckian academicians from continuing his imaginary natural and social history. They were seeking not scientific truth, but professorial degrees.

What I am doing with my presentation of the epoch of "no

marriage" is just that: taking the history of marriage back to the time when it was not in existence at all, not even in its first form. Once I reach that remote epoch I must use other terms and designations, for how can I describe a system in which marriage was not yet born in marriage terms?

Some of these premarriage terms are already in existence. But they are not widely disseminated, are still treated gingerly, and are still wrapped in obscurity and "mystery." For example, how many people know about the stage of "cross-cousin" mating as the transitional form of marriage which preceded matrilocal marriage? And what came before cross-cousin mating? My answer is, as I shall show, sex exchange. And before sex exchange, the sex mate was the "stranger-enemy" that Comrade McGowan is so incensed about.

It is quite valid for Comrade McGowan to demand further information and proof of these propositions and to want to know how the stranger-enemy ultimately became the husband-father. Indeed, I shall also show how the stranger-enemy also became the God. It is also valid to raise the question of the "dual organization," for this was a decisive part of the process. I shall deal in detail on the question of how the dual organization arose out of the split of the primal horde into two moieties and how this was the beginning of a system of *exchange relations* which led, on the one hand, to the expansion of the labor fraternity, and on the other, to cross-cousin mating and finally marriage. But this exposition of exchange relations is new; so far as I know, it does not appear in the existing books on anthropology.

I am only too eager to set down the answers to these questions, but it is a question of time since this is not the only work I am occupied with. However, I can assure Comrade McGowan that this presentation will be made as soon as possible and perhaps I may even convince her of its validity and correctness.

To do this job, however, I shall be obliged to deal with the basic question of *social origins*. And this is another aspect of the study that is repugnant to Comrade McGowan. She refers to this in her introduction, when she speaks of an exchange of correspondence between us a year and half ago, when she warned me that "it was *impossible* to either *start* or to *stop* with social origins" (her emphasis).

I do not propose to stop with the question of social origins, but I do propose to *start* with it. And this will collide with her theory that there was no primeval or subhuman stage of humanity. Comrade McGowan, if I understand her correctly, is challenging not only the Darwinian theory of the evolution of man out of the animal kingdom but the whole bourgeois, not to speak of Marxist, school of archaeologists and historians who subscribe to the Darwinian theory.

Understanding that in this study of social origins, I shall take up where Briffault left off, Comrade McGowan challenges us both with the following vulgarization of certain propositions:

> The solution to their dilemma, according to Robert Briffault and other supporters of the matriarchal theory, goes something as follows: the mothers and sisters looked around for some other herd in the same fix and between the two of them, they thrashed out this burning problem on which the fate of humanity depended. Thus it was that a "founding convention of humanity" was called, the purpose of which was to unite two otherwise warring animal groups. . . . And so it is that the human race ceases to be animal and becomes human by a convention decree.

If Comrade McGowan will refer back to my article, she will find that I did not mention any convention decrees—nor, indeed, any other teleological proposition that the first social cell was organized through conscious contract. What I said was that humanity was driven by *needs;* the biological needs of food and sex and the social need to form the labor collective. I stated that the primal horde arose through the biological avenue of *maternity* and the social avenue of *labor.* These are not my theories; the first is that of Briffault, the second that of Engels. I am only using these theories as the foundation stones of my work. Where do you stand, Comrade McGowan, on these two basic theories? Are you in agreement with them or not?

The reactionary anthropologists are against Engels, Morgan, and Briffault. Where do you stand, Comrade McGowan? The same reactionary anthropologists uphold the twin myths of bourgeois society: (1) That class society is a permanent fixture. (2) That its institutions of marriage and the individual family are also permanent fixtures. Where do you stand, Comrade McGowan? Do you reject both propositions, or only one? Or neither? Let us settle this question of theory, and of *methods and aims,* before we proceed to the fine points in the science of anthropology.

Comrade McGowan is surprised and even pained at my insistence upon pursuing this dangerous study of social origins and the institutions of marriage and the family. It is obvious that I am embarked on a course that can only undermine capitalist myths, prejudices, and institutions. And so she asks: "To what purpose, Comrade Reed?"

My purpose is clear from my method. It is to completely expose the bourgeois myth that this foul system of capitalism existed for all time and will continue to exist for all time, through historical proof. It is to cast illumination upon the magnificent history of labor from the very beginning of human time, and the vital role played in it by the women. It is to tell the workers of today that labor came out of a socialist system and is going forward to a new and higher socialist system. It is to encourage the workers in the task of conquering the colossal dangers they face today by showing how our ancestors conquered equally colossal dangers in the past. It is to demonstrate that the modern oppressed, sick, and anguished family structure will be replaced by new forms of sexual and reproductive relationships corresponding to a new and better society. These and other interesting and important data are my aims and goal.

Perhaps it is in order to ask Comrade McGowan: What do *you* propose to demonstrate through your study of the science of anthropology? What is your method, your aims, your goal?

It is commonly supposed that the science of anthropology is a very lofty, esoteric science, relegated to the special province of special professors and intellectuals and forever beyond the grasp of the average working men and women. This is not true. Like any science, of course, anthropology has its special aspects, difficulties, terminology, etc., and requires study.

But beyond this, there is a special reason why the ruling class and its professorial watchdogs do not wish working people, and by the same token, Marxist social scientists, to have anything much to do with this science. The reason is—it is loaded with social and political dynamite. And it is loaded against the ruling class, its institutions, its myths, its propaganda, and obscurantism. That is why Engels, Morgan, Briffault are so hated by those who uphold and perpetuate the sacred rights of private property and the exploitation of the working class. To uncover the true history of human society and of labor contained in this science would be to deal a powerful blow against the whole capitalist system and its reactionary church.

That is one side of the picture. On the other side, the science of anthropology covers the prehistorical epoch of human social history, that is, before written history came into existence. This history can only be reconstructed and restored through a system of logic. Even more, not any kind of logic, but the Marxist dialectical logic. Thus, in the final analysis, it will be the Marxists, or those who approach them most closely in *method* who will ultimately crack the "secrets" and "riddles" that the reactionary anthropologists declare can never be understood, and reconstruct the ancient history of mankind. That is why *method* is of such decisive importance. And that is why there is such an immediate reaction against this method, whenever it is applied even to the smallest degree by the bourgeois academicians.

Thus, over and above the natural difficulties inherent in the science itself, there exists this added difficulty of the collision between two polar opposite *class* points of view. To enter the field of anthropology is to enter the field of ideological class struggle.

Notes

Introduction

1. The above figures are from U.S. Bureau of the Census, *Statistical Abstract of the United States: 1985* (105th edition.) Washington D.C., 1984.

2. In the first volume of *Capital,* Karl Marx explained the factors that determine the value of workers' labor power in the following terms:

"The value of labour-power is determined, as in the case of every other commodity, by the labour-time necessary for the production, and consequently also the reproduction, of this specific article. In so far as it has value, it represents no more than a definite quantity of the average social labour objectified in it. Labour-power exists only as a capacity of the living individual. Its production consequently presupposes his existence. Given the existence of the individual, the production of labour-power consists in his reproduction of himself or his maintenance. For his maintenance he requires a certain quantity of the means of subsistence. Therefore the labour-time necessary for the production of labour-power is the same as that necessary for the production of those means of subsistence; in other words, the value of labour-power is the value of the means of subsistence necessary for the maintenance of its owner. However, labour-power becomes a reality only by being expressed; it is activated only through labour. But in the course of this activity, i.e., labour, a definite quantity of human muscle, nerve, brain, etc. is expended, and these things have to be replaced. Since more is expended, more must be received. If the owner of labour-power works today, tomorrow he must again be able to repeat the same process in the same conditions as regards health and strength. His means of subsistence must therefore be sufficient to maintain him in his normal state as a working individual. His natural needs, such as food, clothing, fuel and housing vary according to the climatic and other physical peculiarities of his country. On the other hand, the number and extent of his so-called necessary requirements, as also the manner in which they are satisfied, are themselves products of history, and depend therefore to a great extent on the level of civilization attained by a country; in particular they depend on the conditions in which, and consequently on the habits and expectations with which, the class of free workers has been formed. In contrast, therefore, with the case of other commodities, the determination of the value of labour-power contains a historical and moral element. Nevertheless, in a given country at a given period, the average amount of the means of subsistence necessary for the worker is a known *datum*." (Karl Marx, *Capital* [New York: Random House, 1977], vol. 1, pp. 274–75.)

To this we can add the observation that the value of women's labor power under capitalism is invariably less than that of men. In the United States this is reflected in the fact that full-time female workers, taken as a whole, receive 59 cents for every dollar earned by full-time male workers. This inequality is part of the "historical and moral element" that Marx refers to in the determination of the value of labor power. It is due to the legacy of women's oppression throughout the history of class society, which is based on women's economic dependence on men. This dependence begins to break down as soon as women begin to be incorporated into the capitalist labor market. But eliminating the historic legacy and creating the social and economic conditions for real equality between men and women can only be accomplished through complete incorporation of women into economic production and the socialization of domestic work. These goals cannot be completely achieved short of the victorious working-class struggle to overturn capitalist property relations on a world scale.

3. "The Myth of Women's Inferiority" is available in *Problems of Women's Liberation* (New York: Pathfinder Press, 1970). For a later and more thorough treatment of the views advanced in "Sex and Labor in Primitive Society," see Evelyn Reed's *Woman's Evolution* (New York: Pathfinder Press, 1975).

1. From the pages of the 'Militant'

4. The slogan "skin you love to touch" is from a Jergens cosmetics ad in the early 1950s.

5. In 1929 the Communist International (Comintern) proclaimed that world capitalism had entered its "third period," the period of its final collapse. This was a political rationalization for the ultraleft sectarian course initiated under Stalin's leadership both in the Soviet Union and in the Comintern and its parties around the world. The Stalinists branded the Social Democracy as "social fascist," opposed joint action with parties and trade unions under Social Democratic leadership, and abandoned the fight for united-front action in defense of the interests of workers and their allies. This ultraleft course had its reflection in the cultural policies and social norms promoted by the Communist parties during these years.

2. The discussion in the SWP

6. In the mid-1950s, a clique in the Socialist Workers Party led by Murry Weiss, a member of the Political Committee, sought to expand its influence in the party leadership. The primary banner under which it organized to advance its members in the party— male and female—was a rumor campaign about the alleged "male chauvinism" of others in the party leadership.

7. See *Woman's Evolution*, especially pp. 99–103, 282–95.

8. This quotation is paraphrased from Rudyard Kipling's poem "The Ladies." Its last two lines are "For the Colonel's Lady an' Judy O'Grady / Are sisters under their skins."

9. Barbara "Bobo" Rockefeller was born Jievute Paulekiute in a small coal mining town in Pennsylvania. She married Winthrop Rockefeller in 1948.

10. Antoinette Konikow (1869–1946) was a founding member of

the Socialist Party and later of the Communist Party in the United States. In 1928 she joined the movement that, in 1938, became the Socialist Workers Party. Konikow was one of a very small number of physicians in the United States who spoke out publicly and helped lead the fight for the right to birth control in the early years of this century. In 1923 she authored *Voluntary Motherhood* and in 1928 was arrested for lecturing on sex education.

11. Karl Marx, *Capital* (New York: Vintage, 1977), vol. 1, chapter 1 ("The Commodity"), section 4, pp. 163–77.

12. George V. Plekhanov, *Fundamental Problems of Marxism* (New York: International Publishers, 1980), p. 82.

13. Karl Marx and Frederick Engels, *The Communist Manifesto* (New York: Pathfinder Press, 1970).

3. An exchange on the origins of women's oppression

14. Frederick Engels, *Origin of the Family, Private Property and the State* (New York: Pathfinder Press, 1972). This edition contains Engels's article "The Part Played by Labour in the Transition from Ape to Man," as well as an introduction by Evelyn Reed.

15. Lewis Henry Morgan, an American ethnologist, was the author of *Ancient Society, or Researches in the Lines of Human Progress from Savagery through Barbarism to Civilization* (1877). An edition of Morgan's work was published by N.Y. Labor News in 1978. Engels made extensive use of Morgan's findings in writing *Origin of the Family, Private Property and the State.*

Engels polemicized against Edward Westermarck in *Origins of the Family,* pp. 48–51, 62. Westermarck published *History of Human Marriage* in 1891.

For more information on the Marxist method in analyzing anthropological data, see Evelyn Reed's articles "Women and the Family" in *Problems of Women's Liberation* and "Evolutionism and Anti-evolutionism" in *Sexism and Science* (New York: Pathfinder Press, 1978).

Other works by the authors
from Pathfinder Press

Joseph Hansen
Dynamics of the Cuban Revolution
The Leninist Strategy of Party Building:
    The Debate on Guerrilla Warfare in Latin America
The Workers and Farmers Government

Evelyn Reed
Problems of Women's Liberation
Sexism and Science
Woman's Evolution

Mary-Alice Waters
Communism and the Fight for a Popular Revolutionary
    Government: 1848 to Today
Feminism and the Marxist Movement
Rosa Luxemburg Speaks (editor)
Women and the Socialist Revolution

Index

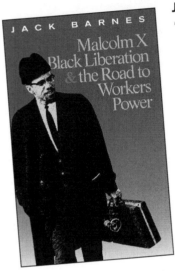

New International

A MAGAZINE OF MARXIST POLITICS AND THEORY

NEW INTERNATIONAL NO. 12

CAPITALISM'S LONG HOT WINTER HAS BEGUN

Jack Barnes

and "Their Transformation and Ours," Resolution of the Socialist Workers Party

Today's sharpening interimperialist conflicts are fueled both by the opening stages of what will be decades of economic, financial, and social convulsions and class battles, and by the most far-reaching shift in Washington's military policy and organization since the US buildup toward World War II. Class-struggle-minded working people must face this historic turning point for imperialism, and draw satisfaction from being "in their face" as we chart a revolutionary course to confront it. $16. Also in Spanish, French, and Swedish. *Capitalism's Long Hot Winter Has Begun* is available in Arabic.

NEW INTERNATIONAL NO. 13

OUR POLITICS START WITH THE WORLD

Jack Barnes

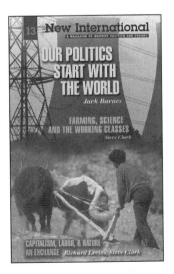

The huge economic and cultural inequalities between imperialist and semicolonial countries, and among classes within almost every country, are produced, reproduced, and accentuated by the workings of capitalism. For vanguard workers to build parties able to lead a successful revolutionary struggle for power in our own countries, says Jack Barnes in the lead article, our activity must be guided by a strategy to close this gap. *Also in No. 13:* "Farming, Science, and the Working Classes" *by Steve Clark.* $14. Also in Spanish, French, and Swedish.

WWW.PATHFINDERPRESS.COM

Women's Liberation and Socialism

Woman's Evolution
From Matriarchal Clan to Patriarchal Family
Evelyn Reed

Assesses women's leading and still largely unknown contributions to the development of human civilization and refutes the myth that women have always been subordinate to men. "Certain to become a classic text in women's history" —Publishers Weekly. $32

Feminism and the Marxist Movement
Mary-Alice Waters

Since the founding of the modern revolutionary workers movement nearly 150 years ago, Marxists have championed the struggle for women's rights and explained the economic roots in class society of women's oppression. "The struggle for women's liberation," Waters writes, "was lifted out of the realm of the personal, the 'impossible dream,' and unbreakably linked to the progressive forces of our epoch"—the working-class struggle for power. $6

Abortion is a Woman's Right!
Pat Grogan, Evelyn Reed

Why abortion rights are central not only to the fight for the full emancipation of women, but to forging a united and fighting labor movement. $6. Also in Spanish.

Problems of Women's Liberation
Evelyn Reed
Six articles explore the social and economic roots of women's oppression from prehistoric society to modern capitalism and point the road forward to emancipation. $15

Women and the Family
Leon Trotsky
How the October 1917 Russian Revolution, the first victorious socialist revolution, transformed the fight for women's emancipation. Trotsky explains the Bolshevik government's steps to wipe out illiteracy, establish equality in economic and political life, set up child-care centers and public kitchens, guarantee the right to abortion and divorce, and more. $13

Communist Continuity and the Fight for Women's Liberation
Documents of the Socialist Workers Party 1971–86
Edited with an introduction
by Mary-Alice Waters

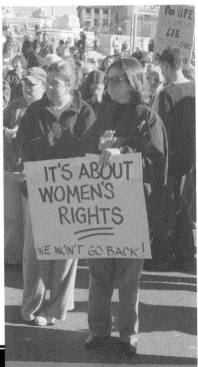

How did the oppression of women begin? What class benefits? What social forces have the power to end the second-class status of women? Why is defense of a woman's right to choose abortion a pressing issue for the labor movement? This three-part series helps politically equip the generation of women and men joining battles in defense of women's rights today. 3 volumes. $30

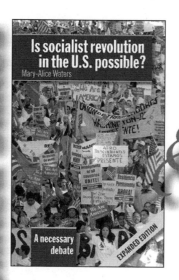

Is Socialist Revolution in the U.S. Possible?

A Necessary Debate

MARY-ALICE WATERS

"To think a socialist revolution in the US is not possible, you'd have to believe not only that the wealthy ruling families and their economic wizards have found a way to 'manage' capitalism. You'd have to close your eyes to the spreading imperialist wars and economic, financial, and social crises we are in the midst of." —Mary-Alice Waters.

In talks given as part of a wide-ranging debate at the 2007 and 2008 Venezuela Book Fairs, Waters explains why a socialist revolution is not only possible, but why revolutionary struggles by working people are inevitable— battles forced on us by the rulers' crisis-driven assaults on our living and job conditions, on our very humanity. $7. Also in Spanish, French, and Swedish.

Cuba and the Coming American Revolution

JACK BARNES

The Cuban Revolution of 1959 had a worldwide political impact, including on working people and youth in the US. In the early 1960s, says Barnes, "the mass proletarian-based struggle to bring down Jim Crow segregation in the South was marching toward bloody victories as the Cuban Revolution was advancing." The deep-going social transformation Cuban toilers fought for and won set an example that socialist revolution is not only necessary— it can be made and defended by workers and farmers in the imperialist heartland as well. Foreword by Mary-Alice Waters. $10. Also in Spanish and French.

The Struggle for a Proletarian Party

JAMES P. CANNON

"The workers of America have power enough to topple the structure of capitalism at home and to lift the whole world with them when they rise," Cannon asserts. On the eve of World War II, a founder of the communist movement in the US and leader of the Communist International in Lenin's time defends the program and party-building norms of Bolshevism. $22

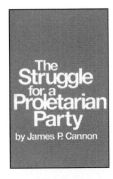

Fighting Racism in World War II

From the Pages of the Militant

An account from 1939 to 1945 of struggles against racism and lynch-mob terror in face of patriotic appeals to postpone resistance until after US "victory" in World War II. These struggles—of a piece with anti-imperialist battles the world over—helped lay the basis for the mass Black rights movement in the 1950s and '60s. $25

The First Ten Years of American Communism

JAMES P. CANNON

A founding leader of the communist movement in the US recounts early efforts to build a proletarian party emulating the Bolshevik leadership of the October 1917 revolution in Russia. $22

Revolutionary Continuity

Marxist Leadership in the U.S.
FARRELL DOBBS

How successive generations of fighters joined in struggles that shaped the US labor movement, seeking to build a revolutionary leadership able to advance the interests of workers and small farmers and link up with fellow toilers worldwide. 2 vols. *The Early Years: 1848–1917*, $20; *Birth of the Communist Movement: 1918–1922*, $19.

Class Struggle in the United States

From the dictatorship of capital...

KARL MARX
FREDERICK ENGELS
The COMMUNIST MANIFESTO
8 HOURS LABOR
INTRODUCTION BY LEON TROTSKY

The Communist Manifesto

Karl Marx, Frederick Engels

Founding document of the modern revolutionary workers movement, published in 1848. Why communism is not a set of preconceived principles but the line of march of the working class toward power—a line of march "springing from an existing class struggle, a historical movement going on under our very eyes." $5. Also in Spanish, French, and Arabic.

State and Revolution

V.I. Lenin

"The relation of the socialist proletarian revolution to the state is acquiring not only practical political importance," wrote V.I. Lenin in this booklet just months before the October 1917 Russian Revolution. It also addresses the "most urgent problem of the day: explaining to the masses what they will have to do to free themselves from capitalist tyranny." In *Essential Works of Lenin*. $12.95

Their Trotsky and Ours

Jack Barnes

To lead the working class in a successful revolution, a mass proletarian party is needed whose cadres, well beforehand, have absorbed a world communist program, are proletarian in life and work, derive deep satisfaction from doing politics, and have forged a leadership with an acute sense of what to do next. This book is about building such a party. $16. Also in Spanish and French.

JACK BARNES — Their Trotsky and Ours

www.pathfinderpress.com

... to the dictatorship of the proletariat

Lenin's Final Fight
Speeches and Writings, 1922–23
V.I. Lenin

In 1922 and 1923, V.I. Lenin, central leader of the world's first socialist revolution, waged what was to be his last political battle. At stake was whether that revolution would remain on the proletarian course that had brought workers and peasants to power in October 1917—and laid the foundations for a truly worldwide revolutionary movement of toilers organizing to emulate the Bolsheviks' example. $20. Also in Spanish.

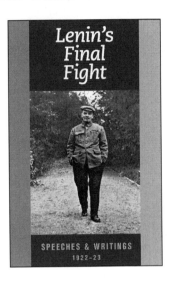

Trade Unions: Their Past, Present, and Future
Karl Marx

Apart from being instruments "required for guerrilla fights between capital and labor," the unions "must now act deliberately as organizing centers of the working class in the broad interest of its complete emancipation," through revolutionary political action. Drafted by Marx for the First International's founding congress in 1866, this resolution appears in *Trade Unions in the Epoch of Imperialist Decay* by Leon Trotsky. $16

The History of the Russian Revolution
Leon Trotsky

The social, economic, and political dynamics of the first socialist revolution as told by one of its central leaders. How, under Lenin's leadership, the Bolshevik Party led the overturn of the monarchist regime of the landlords and capitalists and brought to power a government of the workers and peasants. Unabridged, 3 vols. in one. $38. Also in Russian.

The Cuban Revolution and

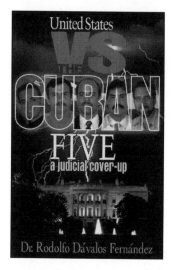

United States vs. The Cuban Five
A Judicial Cover-Up
Rodolfo Dávalos Fernández
Held in US prisons since 1998, five Cuban revolutionists were framed up for being part of a "Cuban spy network" in Florida. They were keeping tabs for Cuban government on rightist groups with a long record of armed attacks on Cuba from US soil. "From start to finish," says the author, court proceedings were "tainted, corrupt, and vindictive. Every right to 'due process of law' was flouted." $22. Also in Spanish.

Episodes of the Cuban Revolutionary War, 1956–58
Ernesto Che Guevara
A firsthand account of the political events and military campaigns that culminated in the January 1959 popular insurrection that overthrew the US-backed dictatorship in Cuba. With clarity and humor, Guevara describes his own political education. He explains how the struggle transformed the men and women of the Rebel Army and July 26 Movement, opening the door to the first socialist revolution in the Americas. $30

Marianas in Combat
Teté Puebla and the Mariana Grajales Women's Platoon in Cuba's Revolutionary War 1956–58
Teté Puebla
Brigadier General Teté Puebla joined the struggle to overthrow the US-backed Batista dictatorship in Cuba in 1956, at age fifteen. This is her story—from clandestine action in the cities, to officer in the Rebel Army's first all-women's platoon. The fight to transform the social and economic status of women is inseparable from Cuba's socialist revolution. $14. Also in Spanish.

World Politics

Soldier of the Cuban Revolution
From the Cane Fields of Oriente
to General in the Revolutionary Armed Forces
Luis Alfonso Zayas

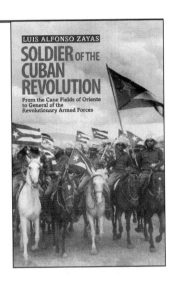

The author recounts his experiences over five decades in the revolution. From a teenage combatant in the clandestine struggle and 1956–58 war that brought down the US-backed dictatorship, to serving three times as a leader of the Cuban volunteer forces that helped Angola defeat an invasion by the army of white-supremacist South Africa, Zayas tells how he and other ordinary men and women in Cuba changed the course of history and, in the process, transformed themselves as well. $18. Also in Spanish.

Our History Is Still Being Written
The Story of Three Chinese-Cuban Generals
in the Cuban Revolution

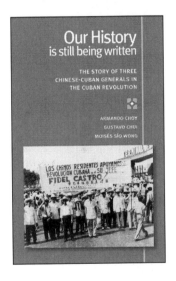

Armando Choy, Gustavo Chui, and Moisés Sío Wong talk about the historic place of Chinese immigration to Cuba, as well as more than five decades of revolutionary action and internationalism, from Cuba to Angola and Venezuela today. Through their stories we see how millions of ordinary men and women opened the door to socialist revolution in the Americas, changed the course of history, and became different human beings in the process. $20. Also in Spanish and Chinese.

Dynamics of the Cuban Revolution
A Marxist Appreciation
Joseph Hansen

How did the Cuban Revolution unfold? Why does it represent an "unbearable challenge" to US imperialism? What political obstacles has it overcome? Written as the revolution advanced from its earliest days. $25

www.pathfinderpress.com

EXPAND *your Revolutionary Library*

The Working Class and the Transformation of Learning
The Fraud of Education Reform under Capitalism
JACK BARNES

"Until society is reorganized so that education is a human activity from the time we are very young until the time we die, there will be no education worthy of working, creating humanity." $3. Also in Spanish, French, Swedish, Icelandic, Farsi, and Greek.

We Are Heirs of the World's Revolutions
Speeches from the Burkina Faso Revolution 1983–87
THOMAS SANKARA

How peasants and workers in this West African country established a popular revolutionary government and began to fight hunger, illiteracy and economic backwardness imposed by imperialist domination, and the oppression of women inherited from class society. They set an example not only for workers and small farmers in Africa, but those the world over. $10. Also in Spanish and French.

America's Revolutionary Heritage
EDITED BY GEORGE NOVACK

A historical materialist analysis of the genocide against Native Americans, the American Revolution, the Civil War, the rise of industrial capitalism, and the first wave of the fight for women's rights. $25

www.pathfinderpress.com

Malcolm X Talks to Young People

"You're living at a time of revolution," Malcolm told young people in the United Kingdom in December 1964. "And I for one will join in with anyone, I don't care what color you are, as long as you want to change the miserable condition that exists on this earth." Four talks and an interview given to young people in Ghana, the UK, and the United States in the last months of Malcolm's life. $15. Also in Spanish and French.

Capitalism and the Transformation of Africa
Reports from Equatorial Guinea

MARY-ALICE WATERS, MARTÍN KOPPEL

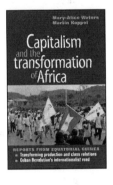

An account of the transformation of class relations in this Central African country, as it is drawn deeper into the world market and both a capitalist class and modern proletariat are born. The example of Cuba's socialist revolution comes alive in the collaboration of Cuban volunteer medical brigades there. Woven together, the outlines of a future to be fought for today can be seen—a future in which Africa's toilers have more weight in world politics than ever before. $10. Also in Spanish.

The Jewish Question
A Marxist Interpretation

ABRAM LEON

Traces the historical rationalizations of anti-Semitism to the fact that, in the centuries preceding the domination of industrial capitalism, Jews emerged as a "people-class" of merchants, moneylenders, and traders. Leon explains why the propertied rulers incite renewed Jew-hatred in the epoch of capitalism's decline. $22

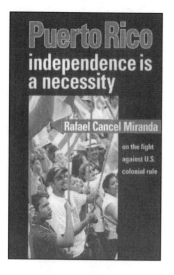

Puerto Rico:
Independence Is a Necessity

RAFAEL CANCEL MIRANDA

One of the five Puerto Rican Nationalists imprisoned by Washington for more than 25 years until 1979 speaks out on the brutal reality of US colonial domination, the campaign to free Puerto Rican political prisoners, the example of Cuba's socialist revolution, and the ongoing struggle for independence. $6. Also in Spanish.

Black Music, White Business
Illuminating the History and Political Economy of Jazz

FRANK KOFSKY

Probes the economic and social conflicts between the artistry of Black musicians and the control by largely white-owned businesses of jazz distribution—the recording companies, booking agencies, festivals, clubs, and magazines. $17

Understanding History
Marxist Essays

GEORGE NOVACK

How did capitalism arise? Why and when did this exploitative system exhaust its potential to advance civilization? Why revolutionary change is fundamental to human progress. $20